Contents

Introduction	6
Choosing a Chicken	8
Cuts of Chicken	8
Techniques	9
Soups, Appetizers & Salads	12
Pasta, Pizza & Rice	26
Stir-fries, Grills, Sautés & Bakes	42
Chicken Roasts, Casseroles & Pies	62
Low-fat Chicken	80
Index	94

Introduction

Chicken is an extremely popular food. It is versatile and economical, and can be cooked with a wide variety of ingredients and flavorings. It is low in fat and quick to cook, with very little wastage.

Chicken can be bought in many forms: whole, quartered or divided into thighs, drumsticks, breasts and wings, with or without bones and skin, which makes preparation very easy. Ground chicken can be found at some large supermarkets, but the skinned flesh can be ground quickly at home in a food processor. Although it is convenient to buy portions individually packaged, it can be expensive. It is much cheaper to buy a whole chicken and prepare it yourself, and cheaper still to buy a frozen chicken and defrost it thoroughly before using. The added bonus of a frozen bird are the giblets (neck, heart, liver and gizzard) found inside the cavity, which can be used for making stock. To get the best results from a frozen chicken, let it thaw slowly in a cool place overnight until defrosted.

Many types of chicken are available, such as free-range and corn-fed (with yellow skin), and all are full of flavor. Some have added herbs and flavorings, and others are self-basting with either butter or olive oil injected into the flesh. This helps keep the flesh succulent. Chicken is available all year round, although some of the more expensive types are raised only in limited numbers. Baby chickens are called poussins and can be bought to serve whole or halved, depending on their size and your appetite. In fact, chicken can be bought at any weight ranging from 1 pound to 6 pounds.

When buying, look for a firm, plump bird with no signs of damage to the limbs, flesh or skin. Unwrap the bird, immediately store it in the refrigerator and use as soon as possible, as all poultry deteriorates very rapidly.

This book offers chicken, turkey and duck recipes from all corners of the world and for every occasion, from simple snacks, appetizers and light dishes, through substantial family casseroles, to presentations for entertaining. The book contains five chapters covering soups, snacks and refreshing salads; pasta, pizzas and satisfying rice dishes; roasts, casseroles and pies; stir-fries, sautés and bakes; and delicious low-fat recipes for people who are watching their cholesterol levels or weight—so there is truly something here for every taste and occasion. You need never again be at a loss for an inspiring chicken recipe.

Choosing a Chicken

When choosing a fresh chicken for cooking, it should have a plump breast, and the skin should be creamy in color. The tip of the breastbone should be pliable when pressed. A bird's dressed weight is taken after plucking and drawing, and may include the giblets (neck, gizzard, heart and liver). A frozen chicken must be thawed slowly in the refrigerator or a cool room before cooking. Never try to thaw it in hot water, as this will toughen the flesh.

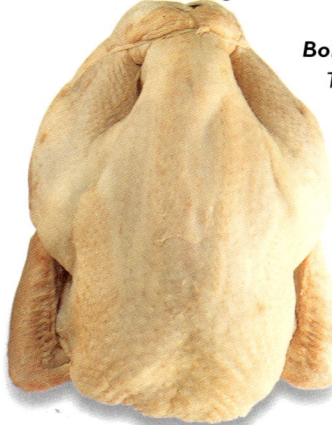

Boilers
These are about 12 months and over, and weigh 4½–6½ pounds. They require long, slow cooking, around 2–3 hours, to make them tender.

Corn-fed Chickens
These are generally more expensive. They usually weigh 2½–3½ pounds.

Roasters
These birds are about 6–12 months old and weigh 3½–4½ pounds. They will feed a family.

Spring Chickens
These birds are about 3 months old and weigh 2–2½ pounds. They will serve three to four people.

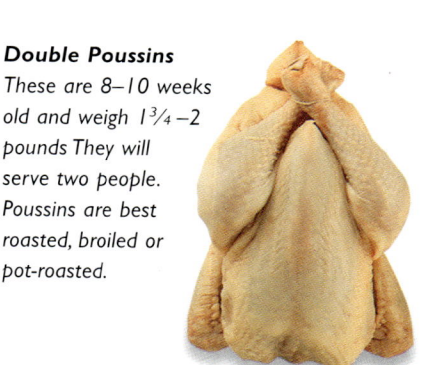

Double Poussins
These are 8–10 weeks old and weigh 1¾–2 pounds They will serve two people. Poussins are best roasted, broiled or pot-roasted.

Poussins
These are 4–6 weeks old and weigh 1–1¼ pounds. They are sufficient for one person.

Cuts of Chicken

Chicken pieces today are available pre-packaged in a variety of different ways. If you do not want to buy a whole bird, you can choose from the many selected cuts on the market. Most cooking methods are suitable for all cuts, but some are especially suited to specific cuts of meat. These are ideal for frying, broiling and grilling.

Skinless Boneless Thigh
This makes tasks such as stuffing and rolling much quicker, as it is already skinned and jointed.

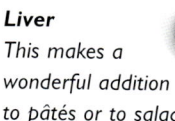

Liver
This makes a wonderful addition to pâtés or to salads.

Ground Chicken
This is not as strongly flavored as, say, ground beef, but may be used as a substitute in some recipes.

Leg
The leg comprises the thigh and drumstick. Large pieces with bones, such as this, are suitable for slow-cooking, such as braising or poaching.

Wing
The wing does not supply much meat. It is often grilled or fried.

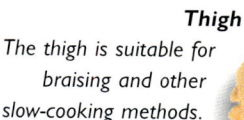

Drumstick
The drumstick is a favorite for grilling or frying, either in batter or rolled in bread crumbs.

Breast
This comprises tender white meat and can be simply cooked in butter, as well as stuffed.

Thigh
The thigh is suitable for braising and other slow-cooking methods.

Techniques

Jointing a Chicken
For recipes that call for chicken joints, it is often cheaper to buy a whole chicken and joint it yourself, particularly if you are cooking for a large number of people. It is important to have a portion of bone with the wing and breast joints, otherwise the flesh shrinks during cooking.

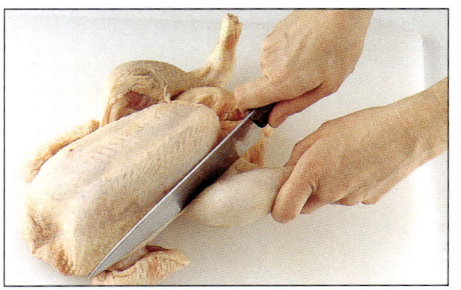

1 Hold the leg firmly with one hand. Using a sharp knife, cut the skin between the leg and breast.

2 Then, press the leg down to expose the ball-and-socket joint, cut or break the joint apart and cut down toward the parson's nose.

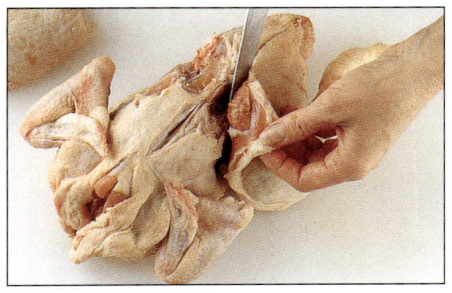

3 Turn the chicken over and loosen the "oyster" from the underside (this lies embedded alongside the backbone). Repeat with the other leg.

4 Now, with your finger, feel for the end of the breastbone, and, using a sharp knife, cut diagonally through the flesh to the rib cage.

5 Using strong kitchen scissors, cut through the rib cage and wishbone, separating the two wing joints.

6 Twist the wing tip and tuck it under the breast meat so that the joint is held flat. This will ensure that it has a good shape for cooking.

7 Using strong kitchen scissors, cut the breast meat from the carcass in one piece. (All that remains of the carcass is half of the rib cage and the backbone.)

8 The legs can be cut in half through the joint to give a thigh joint and a drumstick. The breast can also be cut into two pieces through the breastbone.

Spatchcocking a Chicken
This is a good way to prepare chickens for broiling or grilling, especially the smaller sizes such as poussins. By removing their backbones, poussins can be opened out and flattened, ready for even and fast cooking.

1 Using a very sharp pair of kitchen scissors, cut the poussin on either side of its backbone.

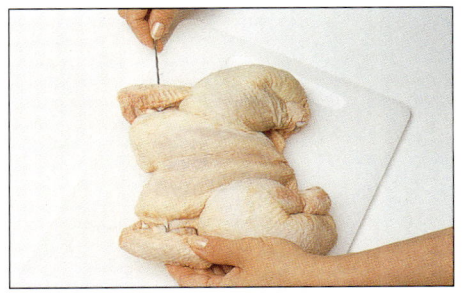

2 Flatten the bird with the palm of your hand or a rolling pin. Turn it over and cut out the fine rib cage, leaving the rest of the carcass intact to hold its shape. Thread thin skewers though the wings.

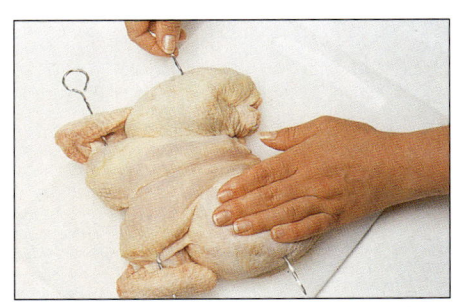

3 Then thread thin skewers through the legs and wings to hold them in position and keep the bird flat. Brush liberally with melted butter. It will take 10–15 minutes on each side, depending on the heat.

Stuffing a Chicken

Stuffing helps keep chickens moist during cooking, which is important because they have very little fat. The stuffing also helps make the meal go further. There are many different flavors of stuffing that may be used to enhance the taste of chicken, without detracting from its own delicate flavor. Bread, rice or potatoes can be used as a base to which other ingredients may be added. Fat is important in stuffing because it prevents it from becoming dry and crumbly.

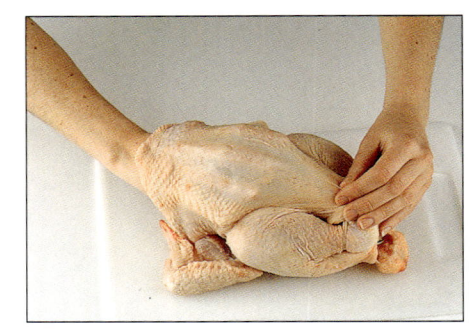

1 Only stuff the small neck-end of the chicken and not the large cavity inside the carcass, as the heat from the oven will not penetrate all the way through the chicken. Any leftover stuffing should be made into small balls and fried separately or put into a shallow, buttered ovenproof dish, baked with the chicken and cut into squares for serving with the chicken.

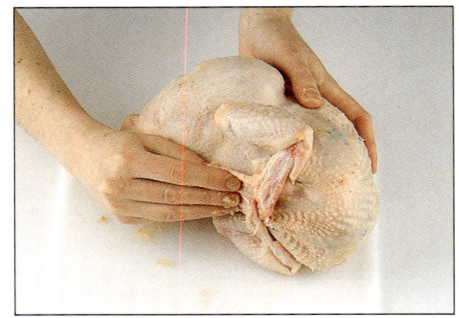

2 Never pack the stuffing too tightly, as bread crumbs will expand during cooking and this may cause the skin to burst open. The flap of neck skin should then be tucked under the chicken and secured with the wing tips or sewn into place with a needle and fine trussing thread. Remember to weigh the chicken after it has been stuffed to calculate the cooking time accurately.

Casseroling

This slow-cooking method is good for large chicken joints with bones, or more mature meat.

1 Heat some olive oil in a flameproof casserole and fry the chicken joints until they are browned on all sides.

2 Add stock, wine or a mixture of both to a depth of 1 inch. Add seasonings and herbs, cover and cook on the stove or in the oven for 1½ hours or until the chicken is tender.

3 Add a selection of lightly fried vegetables such as pearl onions, mushrooms, carrots and small new potatoes about halfway through the cooking time.

Braising

This method can be used for whole chickens or pieces and is ideal for strongly flavored meat.

1 Heat some olive oil in a flameproof casserole and lightly fry a whole bird or chicken joints until golden on all sides.

2 Remove the chicken from the casserole and fry 1 pound diced vegetables, such as carrots, onions, celery and turnips, until soft.

3 Replace the chicken, cover with a tight lid and cook very slowly on the stove or in the oven, preheated to 325°F, until tender.

Carving a Chicken

It is best to let the chicken stand (or "rest") for 10–15 minutes before carving (while the gravy is being made). This lets the meat relax, so the flesh will not tear while carving. Use a sharp carving knife and work on a plate that will catch any juices that can be added to the gravy. The leg can be cut in half for a thigh and a drumstick.

1 Hold the chicken firmly with a carving fork, between the breast and one of the legs, down to the backbone. Cut the skin around the opposite leg, press gently outward to expose the ball-and-socket joint and cut through. Slip the knife under the back to remove the "oyster" with the leg.

2 With the knife at the top end of the breastbone, cut down parallel to one side of the wishbone to take a good slice of breast meat with the wing joint.

3 With the knife at the end of the breastbone, cut down the front of the carcass, removing the wishbone. Carve the remaining breast into slices.

Chicken Stock

A good chicken stock is called for in many dishes, so make a large quantity and freeze it in small batches.

1 onion
4 cloves
1 carrot
2 leeks
2 celery stalks
1 chicken carcass, cooked or raw
1 bouquet garni
8 black peppercorns
½ teaspoon salt

1 Peel the onion, cut into quarters and spike each quarter with a clove. Scrub and roughly chop the other vegetables.

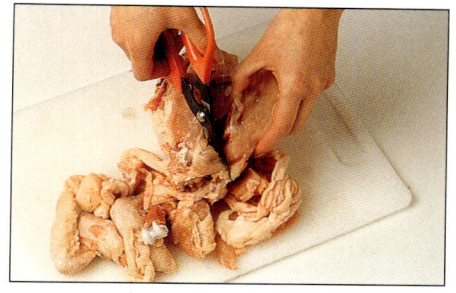

2 Break up the chicken carcass into several pieces and place in a large saucepan with the remaining ingredients.

3 Cover with 7½ cups water. Bring to a boil, skim and simmer, partially covered, for 2 hours. Strain the stock and let cool. When cold, remove the hardened fat before using.

How to Make Gravy

After roasting, transfer the chicken to a serving dish and remove any trussing string. Cover loosely with aluminum foil and let rest in a warm place before carving. Meanwhile, spoon the fat from the juices left in the roasting pan. Stirring constantly, blend 1 tablespoon all-purpose flour into the juices and cook gently on the stove until golden brown. Add 1¼ cups chicken stock or vegetable cooking water and bring to a boil, to thicken. Season to taste. Strain into a pitcher or gravy boat to serve.

Roasting Times for Poultry

Note: Birds should be weighed after stuffing.

Poussin	1–1½ pounds	1–1¼ hours at 350°F
Chicken	2½–3 pounds	1–1¼ hours at 375°F
	3½–4 pounds	1¼–1¾ hours at 375°F
	4½–5 pounds	1½–2 hours at 375°F
	5–6 pounds	1¾–2½ hours at 375°F
Duck	3–5 pounds	1¾–2¼ hours at 400°F
Goose	8–10 pounds	2½–3 hours at 350°F
	10–12 pounds	3–3½ hours at 350°F
Turkey (whole bird)	6–8 pounds	3–3½ hours at 325°F
	8–12 pounds	3–4 hours at 325°F
	12–16 pounds	4–5 hours at 325°F
Turkey (whole breast)	4–6 pounds	1½–2¼ hours at 325°F
	6–8 pounds	2¼–3¼ hours at 325°F

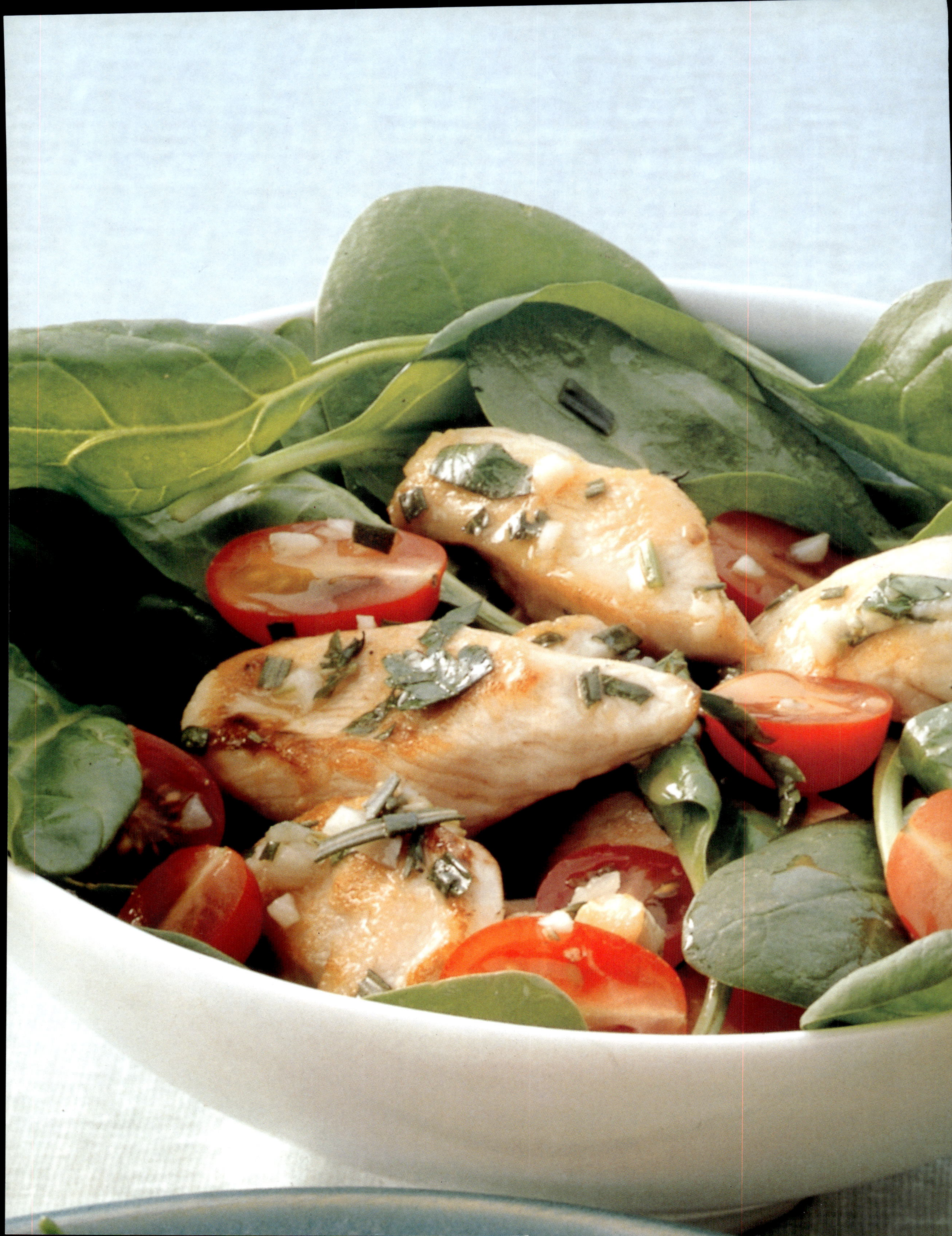

SOUPS, APPETIZERS & SALADS

Chicken Vermicelli Soup

This soup is very quick and easy—you can add all sorts of extra ingredients to vary the taste, using up leftovers.

Serves 4–6
3 large eggs
2 tablespoons chopped cilantro or parsley
6¼ cups Chicken Stock or canned consommé
1 cup dried vermicelli or angel hair pasta
4 ounces cooked chicken breast fillet, sliced
salt and freshly ground black pepper

1 First, make the egg shreds. Whisk the eggs together in a small bowl and stir in the cilantro or parsley.

2 Heat a small, nonstick frying pan and pour in 2–3 tablespoons egg, swirling to cover the bottom evenly. Cook until set. Repeat until all the mixture is used up.

3 Roll up each egg crêpe and slice thinly into shreds using a sharp knife. Set aside until serving.

4 Bring the stock or consommé to a boil in a large saucepan and add the pasta, breaking it up into short lengths. Cook for 3–5 minutes, until the pasta is almost tender, then add the chicken, salt and pepper.

5 Heat through for 2–3 minutes, then stir in the egg shreds. Serve immediately in warmed bowls.

> **Variation**
> To make a Thai variation of this soup, use Chinese rice noodles instead of pasta. Stir ½ teaspoon dried lemongrass, two small whole fresh chiles and ¼ cup coconut milk into the chicken stock or consommé. Add four sliced scallions and chopped cilantro.

Chicken Broth with Cheese Toasts

A really filling, hearty soup that makes excellent use of a chicken carcass and vegetables left over from the weekend roast.

Serves 4
1 roasted chicken carcass
1 onion, quartered
2 celery stalks, finely chopped
1 garlic clove, crushed
a few fresh parsley sprigs
2 bay leaves
8-ounce can chopped tomatoes
7-ounce can chickpeas
2–3 tablespoons leftover vegetables, chopped, or 1 large carrot, finely chopped
1 tablespoon chopped fresh parsley
2 slices toast
¼ cup grated cheese
salt and freshly ground black pepper

1 Pick off any little bits of flesh from the chicken carcass, especially from the underside where there is often some very tasty dark meat. Set aside.

2 Break the carcass in half and place in a large saucepan with the onion, half the celery, the garlic, parsley sprigs, bay leaves and sufficient water to cover. Cover the pan, bring to a boil and simmer for about 30 minutes or until you are left with about 1¼ cups of liquid.

3 Strain the stock and return to the pan. Add the chicken flesh, the remaining celery, the tomatoes, chickpeas (and their liquid), leftover vegetables or carrot and chopped parsley. Season to taste and simmer for another 7–10 minutes.

4 Meanwhile, sprinkle the toast with the cheese and broil until bubbling, then cut into fingers or triangles. Serve the soup hot in warmed bowls with the cheese toasts floating on top or passed separately.

Chicken & Asparagus Soup

A very delicate and delicious soup. When fresh asparagus is not in season, canned white asparagus is an acceptable substitute.

Serves 4
5 ounces chicken breast fillet
1 teaspoon egg white
1 teaspoon cornstarch
4 ounces asparagus
3 cups Chicken Stock
salt and freshly ground
 black pepper
cilantro leaves, to garnish

1 Cut the chicken meat into thin slices, each about the size of a postage stamp. Season with a pinch of salt and stir in the egg white. Mix the cornstarch into a thin paste with a little water and add to the chicken.

2 Trim and discard the tough stems of the asparagus. Diagonally cut the tender spears into short lengths.

3 In a wok or saucepan, bring the stock to a rolling boil. Add the asparagus, return to a boil and cook for 2 minutes. (This is not necessary if using canned asparagus.)

4 Add the chicken, stir to separate and bring back to a boil once more. Taste the soup and adjust the seasoning as necessary. Serve hot, garnished with cilantro leaves.

> **Cook's Tip**
> When buying asparagus, look for tight buds and firm, unwrinkled stems that are evenly colored.

Pasta Soup with Chicken Livers

A soup that can be served as either a first or main course. The fried chicken livers are so delicious that even if you do not normally like them, you will love them in this soup.

Serves 4–6
1 tablespoon olive oil
pat of butter
4 garlic cloves, crushed
3 sprigs each fresh parsley,
 marjoram and sage, chopped
leaves from 1 fresh thyme
 sprig, chopped
5–6 fresh basil leaves, chopped
2/3 cup chicken livers, thawed if
 frozen, cut into small pieces
1–2 tablespoons dry white wine
2 11-ounce cans condensed
 chicken consommé
2 cups frozen peas
1/2 cup small pasta shapes,
 e.g. farfalle
2–3 scallions,
 diagonally sliced
salt and freshly ground
 black pepper
toasted slices of French bread,
 to serve

1 Heat the oil and butter in a frying pan, add the garlic and herbs, with salt and pepper to taste, and sauté gently for a few minutes.

2 Add the livers, increase the heat to high and stir-fry for a few minutes, until they change color and become dry. Pour the wine onto the livers, cook until the wine evaporates, then remove the pan from heat. Season to taste.

3 Pour both cans of condensed chicken consommé into a large saucepan and add water as directed on the labels. Add an extra can of water, season to taste and bring to a boil.

4 Add the peas to the pan and simmer for about 5 minutes, then add the pasta and bring the soup back to a boil, stirring. Simmer, stirring frequently, until the pasta is just *al dente*: about 5 minutes or according to the instructions on the package.

5 Add the fried chicken livers and the scallions, and heat through for 2–3 minutes. Taste and adjust the seasoning as necessary. Serve hot in warm bowls, acccmpanied by toasted slices of French bread.

Chinese Chicken Soup

Corn, scallions, carrots and egg noodles combine with chicken to create this tasty Eastern-style soup.

Serves 4–6
1 tablespoon sesame oil
4 scallions, roughly chopped
8 ounces chicken breast fillet, skinned and cut into small cubes
5 cups Chicken Stock
1 tablespoon soy sauce
1 cup frozen corn kernels
4 ounces medium thread egg noodles
1 carrot
salt and freshly ground black pepper
shrimp crackers, to serve (optional)

1 Heat the oil in a large, heavy saucepan, add the scallions and chicken and cook, stirring constantly, until the meat has browned all over.

2 Pour in the stock and soy sauce, and bring to a boil. Stir in the corn.

3 Add the noodles, breaking them up roughly, and simmer for a few minutes. Season to taste with salt and pepper.

4 Thinly slice the carrot lengthwise. Use small cutters to stamp out shapes from the slices of carrot. Add them to the soup and simmer for 5 minutes.

5 Pour the soup into warmed bowls and serve, accompanied by shrimp crackers if desired.

Chicken & Buckwheat Noodle Soup

This satisfying soup is given body with buckwheat or soba noodles, which are widely enjoyed in Japan.

Serves 4
8 ounces chicken breast fillet, skinned
½ cup soy sauce
1 tablespoon sake
4 cups Chicken Stock
2 pieces young leek, cut into 1-inch pieces
6 ounces spinach leaves
11 ounces buckwheat or soba noodles
sesame seeds, toasted, to garnish

1 Slice the chicken diagonally into bite-size pieces. Combine the soy sauce and sake in a saucepan and bring to a simmer. Add the chicken and cook gently for about 3 minutes, until it is tender. Keep hot.

2 Bring the stock to a boil in another saucepan. Add the leek and simmer for 3 minutes, then add the spinach. Remove from heat but keep warm.

3 Cook the noodles in a large saucepan of boiling water until just tender, following the instructions on the package.

4 Drain the noodles and divide among warmed individual serving bowls. Ladle the hot soup into the bowls, then add a portion of chicken to each. Serve immediately, sprinkled with sesame seeds.

Cook's Tip
Sake is a Japanese rice wine widely available at supermarkets and specialty stores. Do not confuse it with rice vinegar.

Corn & Chicken Soup

This popular classic Chinese soup is delicious and very easy to make.

Serves 4–6

4 ounces chicken breast fillet, skinned and cubed
2 teaspoons light soy sauce
1 tablespoon Chinese rice wine
1 teaspoon cornstarch
1/4 cup cold water
1 teaspoon sesame oil
2 tablespoons peanut oil
1 teaspoon grated fresh ginger root
4 cups Chicken Stock
15-ounce can creamed corn
8-ounce can corn kernels
2 eggs, beaten
2–3 scallions, green parts only, cut into tiny rounds
salt and freshly ground black pepper

1 Grind the chicken in a food processor, taking care not to over-process. Transfer the chicken to a bowl and stir in the soy sauce, rice wine, cornstarch, water, sesame oil and seasoning. Cover and let sit for about 15 minutes to absorb the flavors.

2 Heat a wok over medium heat. Add the peanut oil and swirl it around. Add the ginger and stir-fry for a few seconds. Add the stock, creamed corn and corn kernels. Bring to just below the boiling point.

3 Spoon about 6 tablespoons of the hot liquid into the chicken mixture until it forms a smooth paste, and stir. Return to the wok. Slowly bring to a boil, stirring constantly, then simmer for 2–3 minutes, until cooked.

4 Pour the beaten eggs into the soup in a slow, steady stream, using a fork or chopsticks to stir the top of the soup in a figure-eight pattern. The eggs should set in lacy shreds. Serve immediately in warmed individual soup bowls with the scallions sprinkled on top.

Pumpkin, Rice & Chicken Soup

A warm, comforting soup which, despite the spice and basmati rice, is quintessentially English. For an even more substantial meal, add a little extra rice and make sure you use all the chicken from the stock.

Serves 4

1 pumpkin wedge, about 1 pound
1 tablespoon sunflower oil
2 tablespoons butter
6 green cardamom pods
2 leeks, chopped
1/2 cup basmati rice, soaked in water
1 1/2 cups milk
salt and freshly ground black pepper
generous strips of pared orange zest, to garnish
whole-wheat bread, to serve

For the chicken stock
2 chicken quarters
1 onion, quartered
2 carrots, chopped
1 celery stalk, chopped
6–8 peppercorns
3 3/4 cups water

1 First, to make the chicken stock, place the chicken quarters, onion, carrots, celery and peppercorns in a large saucepan. Pour in the water and bring to a boil over medium heat. Skim the surface if necessary, then lower the heat, cover and simmer gently for 1 hour.

2 Strain the chicken stock into a clean, large bowl, discarding the vegetables. Skin and bone one or both chicken pieces and cut the flesh into strips. (If not using both chicken pieces for the soup, reserve the other piece for another recipe.)

3 Peel the pumpkin, and remove and discard all the seeds and pith, so that you have about 12 ounces flesh. Cut the flesh into 1-inch cubes.

4 Heat the oil and butter in a saucepan and fry the cardamom pods for 2–3 minutes, until slightly swollen. Add the leeks and pumpkin. Cook, stirring, for 3–4 minutes over medium heat, then lower the heat, cover and sweat for 5 more minutes or until the pumpkin is quite tender, stirring once or twice.

5 Measure 2 1/2 cups of the stock and add to the pumpkin mixture. Bring to a boil, lower the heat, cover and simmer for 10–15 minutes, until the pumpkin is soft.

6 Pour the remaining stock into a measuring cup and add water to make 1 1/4 cups. Drain the rice and put it into a saucepan. Pour in the stock, bring to a boil, then simmer for about 10 minutes, until the rice is tender. Add seasoning to taste.

7 Remove the cardamom pods, then process the soup in a blender or food processor until smooth. Pour back into a clean saucepan and stir in the milk, chicken and rice (with any stock that has not been absorbed). Heat until simmering. Pour into warmed bowls and garnish with the strips of pared orange zest and freshly ground black pepper. Serve with whole-wheat bread.

Chicken Soup with Garlic Croutons

A thick, chunky chicken and vegetable soup served with crisp fried croutons: a meal in itself.

Serves 4
4 chicken thighs, boned and skinned
1 tablespoon butter
2 small leeks, thinly sliced
1 tablespoon long-grain rice
3¾ cups Chicken Stock
1 tablespoon mixed chopped fresh parsley and mint
salt and freshly ground black pepper
crusty bread, to serve (optional)

For the garlic croutons
2 tablespoons olive oil
1 garlic clove, crushed
4 slices bread, cut into cubes

1 Cut the chicken into ½-inch cubes. Melt the butter in a saucepan, add the leeks and cook them until they are tender. Add the rice and chicken, and cook for another 2 minutes.

2 Pour in the stock, then cover and simmer for 15–20 minutes or until the rice is cooked and the chicken is tender.

3 To make the garlic croutons, heat the oil in a large frying pan. Add the crushed garlic clove and bread cubes, and cook until golden brown, stirring constantly to prevent burning. Drain on paper towels and sprinkle with a pinch of salt.

4 Add the parsley and mint to the soup and adjust the seasoning to taste. Serve hot in warmed bowls and pass the garlic croutons separately for sprinkling on the soup. Accompany with crusty bread, if desired.

Cock-a-Leekie

This traditional soup recipe—it is known from as long ago as 1598—originally included beef as well as chicken. In the past it would have been made from an old roaster, hence the name.

Serves 4–6
5 cups Chicken Stock
2 chicken portions, about 10 ounces each
1 bouquet garni
4 leeks
8–12 prunes, soaked overnight in water
salt and freshly ground black pepper
buttered soft rolls, to serve

1 Bring the stock to a boil in a large saucepan. Add the chicken and bouquet garni, and simmer gently for 40 minutes.

2 Cut the white part of the leeks into 1-inch slices and thinly slice a little of the green part. Drain the prunes.

3 Add the white parts of the leeks and the prunes to the saucepan and cook gently for 20 minutes, then add the green part of the leeks and cook for another 10–15 minutes.

4 Discard the bouquet garni. Remove the chicken from the pan, discard the skin and bones, and chop the flesh. Return the chicken to the pan and season the soup to taste. Heat the soup through, then serve hot with buttered soft rolls.

> **Cook's Tip**
> Bouquet garni traditionally consists of fresh herbs—usually a bay leaf, thyme sprigs and parsley stalks. Ready-made dried bouquets garnis are also available.

Chicken & Curry Mayonnaise Sandwich

A very useful and appetizing way of using leftover pieces of chicken.

Makes 2
4 slices whole-grain bread
2 tablespoons softened butter
4 ounces cooked chicken, sliced
1 bunch watercress, trimmed

For the curry mayonnaise
½ cup ready-made mayonnaise
2 teaspoons concentrated curry paste
½ teaspoon lemon juice
2 teaspoons sieved apricot jam

1 To make the curry mayonnaise, put all the ingredients in a bowl and mix thoroughly. Chill until needed.

2 Spread the bread with butter and arrange the chicken on two of the slices. Spread curry mayonnaise on the chicken slices.

3 Arrange sprigs of watercress on top, cover with the remaining bread and press lightly together. Cut in half and serve.

> **Variation**
> *For an alternative spicy mayonnaise, add 1 teaspoon English mustard, 1 teaspoon Worcestershire sauce and a dash of Tabasco sauce to the ready-made mayonnaise.*

Asian Chicken Sandwich

This filling is also good served in warmed pita bread—just cut the chicken into small cubes before brushing with the soy mixture, broil on skewers and serve warm.

Makes 2
6 ounces chicken breast fillet, skinned
1 tablespoon soy sauce
1 teaspoon honey
1 teaspoon sesame oil
1 garlic clove, crushed
4 slices white bread
¼ cup peanut sauce
1 ounce bean sprouts
1 ounce red bell pepper, seeded and finely sliced

1 Place the chicken breast in a heatproof dish or roasting pan. Combine the soy sauce, honey, sesame oil and garlic. Brush on the chicken breast.

2 Broil the chicken for 3–4 minutes on each side until cooked through, then slice thinly.

3 Spread two slices of the white bread with some of the peanut sauce.

4 Lay the chicken on the sauce-covered bread.

5 Spread a little more sauce on the chicken.

6 Sprinkle on the bean sprouts and red pepper, and sandwich together with the remaining slices of bread. Serve.

> **Cook's Tip**
> *For homemade peanut sauce, stir together 1 seeded and ground fresh red chile, 2 tablespoons coconut milk and 4 ounces crunchy peanut butter over low heat until thick and smooth. Stir in 1 teaspoon brown sugar, 1 teaspoon lemon juice and salt to taste. Set aside to cool.*

Hot Turkey Sandwich

A generous open sandwich that can be made with leftover roast turkey breast, served with a delicious hot mushroom gravy.

Serves 4
4 tablespoons butter
 or margarine
½ small onion, finely chopped
3 cups button mushrooms,
 quartered
1¼ pounds roast turkey breast
2 cups thick turkey gravy
4 thick slices whole-wheat bread
fresh parsley sprigs, to garnish

1 Melt half the butter or margarine in a frying pan. Add the onion and cook for 5 minutes, until softened.

2 Add the mushrooms and cook for about 5 minutes, stirring occasionally, until the moisture they render has evaporated.

3 Meanwhile, skin the turkey breast and carve the meat into four thick slices.

4 In a saucepan, heat up the turkey gravy. Stir in the onion and mushroom mixture.

5 Spread the slices of bread with the remaining butter or margarine. Set a slice on each of four plates and top with the turkey slices. Pour the mushroom gravy onto the turkey and serve hot, garnished with parsley.

Variation
If desired, the sandwich bread may be toasted and buttered.

Chinese Duck in Pita

This recipe is based on Chinese crispy duck, but uses duck breast instead of whole duck. After 15 minutes' cooking, the duck breast will still have a pinkish tinge. If you like it well-done, leave it in the oven for another 5 minutes.

Makes 2
1 duck breast, about 6 ounces
3 scallions
3-inch piece cucumber
2 round pita breads
2 tablespoons hoisin sauce
radish chrysanthemum and
 scallion tassel, to garnish

1 Preheat the oven to 425°F. Skin the duck breast, place the skin and breast separately on a rack in a roasting pan and bake for 10 minutes.

2 Remove the skin from the oven, cut into pieces and return to the oven with the breast for another 5 minutes.

3 Meanwhile, cut the scallions and cucumber into fine shreds about 1½ inches long.

4 Heat each pita bread in the oven for a few minutes until puffed up, then split in half to make a pocket. Slice the duck breast thinly.

5 Stuff the duck breast into the pita bread with a little scallion, cucumber, crispy duck skin and some hoisin sauce. Serve, garnished with a radish chrysanthemum and scallion tassel.

Variation
Use Chinese chives instead of scallions and plum sauce instead of hoisin.

Chicken with Lemon & Garlic

This succulent dish is simplicity itself to cook and will disappear from the serving plates even more quickly.

Serves 4
8 ounces chicken breast fillets, skinned
2 tablespoons olive oil
1 shallot, finely chopped
4 garlic cloves, finely chopped
1 teaspoon paprika
juice of 1 lemon
2 tablespoons chopped fresh parsley
salt and freshly ground black pepper
lemon wedges, to serve
flat-leaf parsley, to garnish

1 Sandwich the chicken breast fillets between two sheets of plastic wrap or waxed paper. Beat with a rolling pin until the fillets are about ¼ inch thick, then cut into strips about ½ inch wide.

2 Heat the oil in a large frying pan. Stir-fry the chicken strips with the shallot, garlic and paprika over high heat for about 3 minutes, until lightly browned and cooked through.

3 Add the lemon juice and parsley with salt and pepper to taste. Serve hot with lemon wedges, garnished with flat-leaf parsley.

> **Variation**
> Try using strips of turkey breast instead for this dish.

Nutty Chicken Balls

Serve these as a first course with the lemon sauce, or make into smaller balls and serve on toothpicks as canapés with drinks.

Serves 4
2 ounces boneless chicken
½ cup pistachios, finely chopped
1 tablespoon lemon juice
2 eggs, beaten
all-purpose flour, for shaping
¾ cup blanched chopped almonds
generous 1 cup dried bread crumbs
oil, for greasing
salt and freshly ground black pepper

For the lemon sauce
⅔ cup Chicken Stock
1 cup cream cheese
1 tablespoon lemon juice
1 tablespoon chopped fresh parsley
1 tablespoon snipped fresh chives

1 Skin the chicken and grind or chop finely. Mix with salt and pepper to taste, plus the pistachios, lemon juice and 1 of the beaten eggs.

2 Shape into 16 small balls using floured hands (use a spoon as a guide, so that all the balls are roughly the same size). Roll the balls in the remaining beaten egg and coat with the almonds first and then the dried bread crumbs, pressing on firmly. Chill until ready to cook.

3 Preheat the oven to 375°F. Place the chicken balls on a greased baking sheet and bake for about 15 minutes or until golden brown and crisp.

4 To make the lemon sauce, gently heat the chicken stock and cream cheese together in a pan, whisking until smooth. Add the lemon juice, herbs and seasoning to taste. Serve hot with the chicken balls.

Glazed Chicken with Cashews

Hoisin sauce lends a sweet yet slightly hot note to this chicken dish, while cashews add a pleasing contrast of texture.

Serves 4
- ¾ cup cashews
- 1 red bell pepper
- 1 pound chicken breast fillet, skinned
- 3 tablespoons peanut oil
- 4 garlic cloves, finely chopped
- 2 tablespoons rice wine or medium-dry sherry
- 3 tablespoons hoisin sauce
- 2 teaspoons sesame oil
- 5–6 scallions, green parts only, cut into 1-inch lengths
- cooked rice or noodles, to serve

1 Heat a wok or heavy frying pan until hot, add the cashews and stir-fry over low to medium heat for 1–2 minutes, until golden brown. Remove from heat and set the cashews aside.

2 Halve the red pepper and remove the seeds. Slice the pepper and chicken into finger-length strips.

3 Heat the wok again until hot, add the oil and swirl it around. Add the garlic and let it sizzle in the oil for a few seconds. Add the red pepper and chicken, and stir-fry for 2 minutes.

4 Add the rice wine or sherry and hoisin sauce. Continue to stir-fry until the chicken is tender and all the ingredients are evenly glazed.

5 Stir in the sesame oil, reserved toasted cashews and the scallion tips. Serve immediately with rice or noodles.

> **Variation**
> Use blanched almonds instead of cashews if you prefer.

Yellow Chicken

A super-fast version of an all-time Chinese favorite stir-fry.

Serves 4
- 2 tablespoons oil
- ¾ cup salted cashews
- 4 scallions
- 1 pound chicken breast fillet
- 5½-ounce jar yellow bean sauce
- cooked rice, to serve

1 Heat 1 tablespoon of the oil in a wok or frying pan and fry the cashews until browned. Remove from the pan with a slotted spoon and set aside.

2 Roughly chop the scallions. Skin and thinly slice the chicken fillets. Heat the remaining oil and cook the scallions and chicken for 5–8 minutes, until the meat is browned all over and cooked.

3 Return the nuts to the pan and pour on the jar of sauce. Stir well and cook gently until hot. Serve immediately, accompanied by cooked rice.

> **Cook's Tip**
> Yellow bean sauce is made from salted, fermented yellow soybeans crushed with sugar and flour to make a thick paste. It is available at supermarkets and Chinese food stores.

Stir-fried Chicken with Pineapple

An Indonesian-inspired dish in which pineapple adds an extra dimension to chicken and the usual stir-fry flavorings.

Serves 4–6

1¼ pounds chicken breast fillet
2 tablespoons cornstarch
¼ cup sunflower oil
1 garlic clove, crushed
2-inch piece fresh ginger root, peeled and cut into matchsticks
1 small onion, thinly sliced
1 fresh pineapple, peeled, cored and cubed, or 15-ounce can pineapple chunks in natural juice
2 tablespoons dark soy sauce
1 bunch scallions, white bulbs left whole, green tops sliced
salt and freshly ground black pepper

1 Skin the chicken fillets and slice thinly on the diagonal. Toss the strips of chicken in the cornstarch with a little seasoning.

2 Heat the oil in a wok or heavy frying pan and stir-fry the chicken for 5–8 minutes, until lightly browned and cooked through. Lift the chicken out of the wok using a slotted spoon and keep warm.

3 Reheat the oil and sauté the garlic, ginger and onion until soft but not browned. Add the fresh pineapple and ½ cup water, if using, or the canned pineapple pieces together with their juice.

4 Stir in the soy sauce and return the chicken to the pan to heat through. Taste and adjust the seasoning as necessary.

5 Stir in the whole scallion bulbs and half of the sliced green tops. Toss well together and then turn the chicken stir-fry onto a serving platter. Serve garnished with the remaining sliced green scallion tops.

Thai Chicken & Vegetable Stir-fry

An all-in-one main course that needs only boiled or steamed rice as an accompaniment.

Serves 4

2 tablespoons sunflower oil
1 lemongrass stalk, thinly sliced
½-inch piece fresh ginger root, peeled and chopped
1 large garlic clove, chopped
10 ounces lean chicken, thinly sliced
½ red bell pepper, seeded and sliced
½ green bell pepper, seeded and sliced
4 scallions, chopped
2 medium carrots, cut into matchsticks
¾ cup fine green beans
2 tablespoons oyster sauce
pinch of sugar
salt and freshly ground black pepper
¼ cup salted peanuts, lightly crushed, and cilantro leaves, to garnish
cooked rice, to serve

1 Heat the oil in a wok or heavy frying pan over high heat. Add the lemongrass, ginger and garlic, and stir-fry for 30 seconds, until lightly browned.

2 Add the chicken and stir-fry for 2 minutes. Then add the vegetables and stir-fry for 4–5 minutes, until the chicken is cooked and the vegetables are almost cooked.

3 Stir in the oyster sauce, sugar and seasoning to taste, and stir-fry for another minute to mix and blend well.

4 Serve immediately, sprinkled with the peanuts and cilantro leaves, and accompanied by rice.

Variations

If lemongrass is unavailable, you can substitute the thinly pared and chopped zest of ½ lemon, although the citrus flavor will not be as intense. Make this quick supper dish a little hotter by adding more fresh ginger root, if desired.

Chicken with Snowpeas & Cilantro

Delicate and fresh-tasting snowpeas are excellent in stir-fries and also give additional color to paler ingredients, such as chicken.

Serves 4
4 chicken breast fillets, skinned
8 ounces snowpeas
vegetable oil, for deep-frying
1 tablespoon vegetable oil
3 garlic cloves, finely chopped
1-inch piece fresh ginger root, freshly grated
5–6 scallions, cut into 1½-inch lengths
2 teaspoons sesame oil
2 tablespoons chopped cilantro
salt
cooked rice, to serve

For the marinade
1 teaspoon cornstarch
1 tablespoon light soy sauce
1 tablespoon medium-dry sherry
1 tablespoon vegetable oil

For the sauce
1 teaspoon cornstarch
2–3 teaspoons dark soy sauce
½ cup Chicken Stock
2 tablespoons oyster sauce

1 Cut the chicken into strips about ½ x 1½ inches and place in a wide, shallow dish. To make the marinade, blend the cornstarch and soy sauce in a small bowl. Stir in the sherry and oil. Pour onto the chicken, turning the pieces to coat them evenly, and set aside for 30 minutes.

2 Trim the snowpeas and plunge into a pan of boiling salted water. Bring back to a boil, then drain and refresh under cold running water.

3 To make the sauce, combine the cornstarch, soy sauce, stock and oyster sauce in a bowl. Set aside.

4 Heat the oil in a deep-fat fryer. Drain the chicken strips and fry, in batches if necessary, for about 30 seconds, until brown. Remove using a slotted spoon and drain on paper towels.

5 Heat 1 tablespoon oil in a wok or heavy frying pan and add the garlic and ginger. Stir-fry for 30 seconds. Add the snowpeas and stir-fry for 1–2 minutes. Transfer to a plate and keep warm.

6 Heat another 1 tablespoon oil in the wok, add the scallions and stir-fry for 1–2 minutes. Add the chicken and stir-fry for 2 minutes. Pour in the sauce, reduce the heat and cook until it thickens and the chicken is cooked through.

7 Return the snowpeas to the wok, and stir in the sesame oil and chopped cilantro. Serve with rice.

> **Variation**
> If snowpeas are not available you could use broccoli or green beans.

Fu-yung Chicken

Because the egg whites (*Fu-yung* in Chinese) mixed with milk are deep-fried, they have prompted some rather imaginative cooks to refer to this dish as "deep-fried milk!"

Serves 4
6 ounces chicken breast fillet
1 teaspoon salt
4 egg whites, lightly beaten
1 tablespoon cornstarch
2 tablespoons milk
vegetable oil, for deep-frying
1 lettuce heart, separated into leaves
about ½ cup Chicken Stock
1 tablespoon Chinese rice wine or dry sherry
1 tablespoon peas
few drops of sesame oil
1 teaspoon very finely chopped ham, to garnish

1 Finely grind the chicken meat and place in a bowl. Add a pinch of the salt and the egg whites. Mix the cornstarch into a thin paste with a little water and add to the bowl with the milk. Blend well until smooth.

2 Heat the oil in a very hot wok, but before the oil gets too hot, gently spoon the chicken mixture into the oil in batches. Do not stir, otherwise it will spatter. Stir the oil from the bottom of the wok so that the chicken pieces rise to the surface. Remove the chicken as soon as the color turns bright white. Drain.

3 Pour off the excess oil, leaving about 1 tablespoon in the wok. Add the lettuce leaves and remaining salt, and stir-fry for 1 minute. Add the stock and bring to a boil.

4 Return the chicken to the wok, add the rice wine or sherry and peas, and blend well. Sprinkle with the sesame oil, garnish with the ham and serve.

Shredded Chicken with Celery

The tender chicken breast makes a fine contrast with the crisp texture of the celery, and the red chiles add color and flavor.

Serves 4

10 ounces chicken breast fillet, skinned
1 teaspoon salt
½ egg white, lightly beaten
2 teaspoons cornstarch
about 2 cups vegetable oil
1 celery heart, thinly shredded
1–2 fresh red chiles, seeded and thinly shredded
1 scallion, thinly shredded
few strips of fresh ginger root, peeled and thinly shredded
1 teaspoon light brown sugar
1 tablespoon Chinese rice wine or dry sherry
few drops of sesame oil

1 Using a sharp knife, thinly shred the chicken. Place in a bowl and add a pinch of the salt and the egg white. Mix the cornstarch into a thin paste with a little water and add to the bowl, stirring well to coat.

2 Heat the oil in a wok or heavy frying pan until warm, add the chicken and stir to separate the shreds. When the chicken turns white, remove with a slotted spoon and drain on paper towels. Keep warm.

3 Pour all but 2 tablespoons of the oil from the wok. Add the celery, chiles, scallion and ginger, and stir-fry for 1 minute.

4 Return the chicken to the wok and add the remaining salt, sugar and rice wine or sherry. Stir-fry for 1 minute, then add the sesame oil. Serve immediately.

Cook's Tip
Sesame oil is not often used for frying in Chinese cooking. It is usually added toward the end of the cooking time to provide extra flavor.

Chicken with Chinese Vegetables

Shiitake mushrooms, bamboo shoots and snowpeas combine with chicken in this tasty stir-fry.

Serves 4

8–10 ounces chicken, boned and skinned
1 teaspoon salt
½ egg white, lightly beaten
2 teaspoons cornstarch
¼ cup vegetable oil
6–8 small dried shiitake mushrooms, soaked in water and drained
4 ounces canned sliced bamboo shoots, drained
4 ounces snowpeas, trimmed
1 scallion, cut into short sections
few small pieces of fresh ginger root, peeled
1 teaspoon light brown sugar
1 tablespoon light soy sauce
1 tablespoon Chinese rice wine or dry sherry
few drops of sesame oil

1 Using a sharp knife, cut the chicken into thin slices, each about the size of an oblong postage stamp. Place in a bowl and mix with a pinch of the salt and the egg white. Mix the cornstarch into a thin paste with a little water and add to the bowl.

2 Heat a wok or heavy frying pan and add the oil. When the oil is hot, add the chicken and stir-fry over medium heat for about 30 seconds, then remove with a slotted spoon and drain on paper towels. Keep warm.

3 Add the mushrooms, bamboo shoots, snowpeas, scallion and ginger to the wok, and stir-fry over high heat for about 1 minute.

4 Return the chicken to the wok, and add the remaining salt and the sugar. Blend, then add the soy sauce and rice wine or sherry. Stir a few more times. Sprinkle with the sesame oil and serve immediately.

Sweet-&-Sour Kebabs

This marinade contains sugar and will burn very easily, so grill the kebabs slowly, turning often. Serve with harlequin rice.

Serves 2
2 chicken breast fillets, skinned
8 pickling onions or 2 medium onions, peeled
4 strips bacon
3 firm bananas
1 red bell pepper, seeded and diced
flat-leaf parsley sprig, to garnish

For the marinade
2 tablespoons soft brown sugar
1 tablespoon Worcestershire sauce
2 tablespoons lemon juice
salt and freshly ground black pepper

1 To make the marinade, combine ingredients in a bowl. Cut each chicken breast into four pieces, add to the marinade, cover and refrigerate for at least 4 hours or preferably overnight.

2 Blanch the onions in boiling water for 5 minutes and drain. If using medium onions, quarter them after blanching.

3 Cut each strip of bacon in half. Peel the bananas and cut each into three pieces. Wrap a strip of bacon around each piece of banana.

4 Thread the bacon-wrapped banana pieces onto metal skewers with the chicken pieces, onions and pepper pieces. Brush with the marinade.

5 Grill over low coals or cook under a preheated broiler for 15 minutes, turning and basting frequently with the marinade. Garnish with parsley and serve.

Cook's Tip
Pour boiling water onto the small onions and then drain, to make peeling easier.

Citrus Kebabs

A piquant orange, lemon and mint marinade with a hint of cumin makes these kebabs special.

Serves 4
4 chicken breast fillets, skinned
fresh mint sprigs and orange, lemon or lime slices, to garnish
salad leaves, to serve

For the marinade
finely grated zest and juice of $\frac{1}{2}$ orange
finely grated zest and juice of $\frac{1}{2}$ small lemon or lime
2 tablespoons olive oil
2 tablespoons honey
2 tablespoons chopped fresh mint
$\frac{1}{4}$ teaspoon ground cumin
salt and freshly ground black pepper

1 Cut the chicken into 1-inch cubes. To make the marinade, combine the ingredients in a bowl. Add the chicken cubes and let marinate for at least 2 hours.

2 Thread the chicken pieces onto metal skewers and grill over low coals or broil under a preheated broiler for 15 minutes, basting with the marinade and turning frequently.

3 Serve the kebabs on a bed of salad leaves, garnished with mint sprigs and orange, lemon or lime slices.

Harlequin Rice

This is a delicious and colorful accompaniment to kebabs.

Serves 4
2 tablespoons olive oil
generous 1 cup cooked rice
1 cup cooked peas
1 small red bell pepper, diced
salt and freshly ground black pepper

1 Heat the oil in a frying pan and add the rice, peas and diced red pepper.

2 Season to taste with salt and pepper. Stir until heated through, then serve immediately.

Chicken Liver Kebabs

These may be broiled and served with rice and broccoli or grilled outdoors and served with salad and baked potatoes.

Serves 4

4 ounces bacon
12 ounces chicken livers, trimmed
12 large pitted prunes
12 cherry tomatoes
8 button mushrooms
2 tablespoons olive oil
mixed green salad, to serve

1 Cut each strip of bacon in half, wrap a piece around each chicken liver and secure in position with wooden toothpicks.

2 Wrap the pitted prunes around the cherry tomatoes.

3 Thread the bacon-wrapped livers onto metal skewers with the prune-wrapped tomatoes and the mushrooms. Brush with oil. Cook under a preheated broiler for 5 minutes on each side. Alternatively, cover the tomatoes and prunes with a strip of aluminum foil to protect them and cook on a hot grill for 5 minutes on each side.

4 Remove the toothpicks from the livers. Serve the kebabs immediately on warmed plates, accompanied by a mixed green salad.

Cook's Tip
Light the grill 30–45 minutes before you intend to cook. The coals will be at the right temperature when they are glowing and covered with a thin layer of grayish-white ash.

Chicken, Bacon & Corn Kebabs

Don't wait for warm weather to have kebabs. If you are serving them to children, remember to remove the skewers first.

Serves 4

2 ears corn
8 thick strips bacon
8 brown cap mushrooms, halved
2 small chicken breast fillets
2 tablespoons sunflower oil
1 tablespoon lemon juice
1 tablespoon maple syrup
salt and freshly ground black pepper
green salad, to serve

1 Cook the corn in boiling water until tender, then drain and cool. Stretch the bacon strips with the back of a heavy knife and cut each in half. Wrap a piece of bacon around each half mushroom.

2 Cut both the corn and chicken into eight equal pieces. Combine the oil, lemon juice, maple syrup and seasoning, and brush liberally on the chicken.

3 Thread the corn, bacon-wrapped mushrooms and chicken pieces alternately on metal skewers and brush all over with the lemon dressing.

4 Broil the kebabs under a preheated broiler for 8–10 minutes, turning them once and basting occasionally with any extra dressing. Serve hot with a crisp green salad.

Cook's Tip
Made from the sap of a North American tree, pure maple syrup is expensive, but its flavor is vastly superior to blended varieties.

Pan-fried Honey Chicken Drumsticks

Flavored with a sweet marinade before frying, these drumsticks are served with a wine sauce.

Serves 4
½ cup honey
juice of 1 lemon
2 tablespoons soy sauce
1 tablespoon sesame seeds
½ teaspoon fresh or dried
  thyme leaves
12 chicken drumsticks
¾ cup all-purpose flour
3 tablespoons butter
  or margarine
3 tablespoons vegetable oil
½ cup white wine
½ cup Chicken Stock
salt and freshly ground
  black pepper
fresh flat-leaf parsley, to garnish

1 In a large bowl, combine the honey, lemon juice, soy sauce, sesame seeds and thyme. Add the chicken drumsticks and mix to coat them well. Let marinate in a cool place for 2 hours or more, turning occasionally.

2 Mix ½ teaspoon each of salt and pepper with the flour in a shallow bowl. Drain the drumsticks, reserving the marinade. Roll them in the seasoned flour to coat all over.

3 Heat the butter or margarine with the oil in a large, heavy frying pan. When hot and sizzling, add the drumsticks and brown on all sides. Reduce the heat to medium-low and cook for 12–15 minutes, until the chicken is done.

4 Check that the chicken is cooked through by piercing the thickest part with a fork: the juices should run clear. Remove the drumsticks from the pan, place on a serving platter and keep hot.

5 Pour off most of the fat from the pan. Add the white wine, chicken stock and reserved marinade, and stir well to mix in the cooking juices on the bottom of the pan. Bring to a boil and simmer until reduced by half. Season to taste, then spoon the sauce onto the drumsticks and serve, garnished with flat-leaf parsley.

Chicken Lollipops

These tasty stuffed wings can be served hot or cold. They can be prepared and frozen in advance.

Makes 12
12 large chicken wings
3 cups dried bread crumbs
2 tablespoons sesame seeds
2 eggs, beaten
oil, for deep-frying

For the filling
1 teaspoon cornstarch
¼ teaspoon salt
½ teaspoon fresh thyme leaves
pinch of freshly ground
  black pepper

1 Remove the wing tips and discard or use them for making stock. Skin the second joint sections, removing the two small bones, and reserve the meat for the filling.

2 To make the filling, place all the ingredients in a bowl and add the reserved chicken meat. Mix well.

3 Holding the large end of the bone on the third section of the wing and using a sharp knife, cut the skin and flesh off the bone, scraping down and pulling the meat over the small end, forming a pocket. Repeat this process with the remaining wing sections.

4 Fill the tiny pockets with the filling. Mix the bread crumbs and the sesame seeds together. Place the bread crumb mixture and the beaten eggs in separate dishes.

5 Brush the meat with beaten egg and roll in the bread crumb mixture to cover. Chill and repeat to give a second layer, forming a thick coating. Chill until ready to fry.

6 Preheat the oven to 350°F. Heat 2 inches oil in a heavy pan until hot but not smoking, or the bread crumbs will burn. Gently fry two or three lollipops at a time until golden brown, remove and drain on paper towels. Complete the cooking for 15–20 minutes or until tender. Serve hot or cold.

Chicken with Sweet Potatoes

Sweet potatoes are still an undervalued vegetable. A dish like this, in which they are baked with chicken and finished with an orange and ginger glaze, shows them at their best.

Serves 6
grated zest and juice of 1 large navel orange
6 tablespoons soy sauce
1-inch piece fresh ginger root, peeled and finely grated
¼ teaspoon pepper
2½ pounds chicken portions
½ cup all-purpose flour
3 tablespoons corn oil
2 tablespoons butter or margarine
2 pounds sweet potatoes, peeled and cut into 1-inch pieces
3 tablespoons light brown sugar
steamed broccoli, to serve

1 In a plastic bag, combine the orange zest and juice, soy sauce, ginger and pepper. Add the chicken pieces. Put the bag in a mixing bowl (this will keep the chicken immersed in the marinade) and seal. Let marinate in the refrigerator overnight.

2 Preheat the oven to 425°F. Drain the chicken, reserving the marinade. Coat the chicken with flour, shaking off any excess.

3 Heat 2 tablespoons of the oil in a frying pan. Add the chicken pieces and brown on all sides. Remove from the pan and drain.

4 Put the remaining oil and the butter or margarine in a 12 × 9-inch ovenproof dish. Briefly heat in the oven.

5 Put the potato pieces in the bottom of the dish, tossing well to coat with the butter and oil. Arrange the chicken portions in a single layer on top of the potatoes. Cover with aluminum foil and bake for 40 minutes.

6 Mix the reserved marinade with the brown sugar. Remove the foil from the baking dish and pour the marinade mixture onto the chicken and potatoes. Bake, uncovered, for about 20 minutes, until the chicken and potatoes are cooked through and tender. Serve with steamed broccoli.

Golden Chicken

One of those rare dishes that is better cooked in advance and reheated. The chicken (preferably an old boiling fowl and not a young roaster) cooks in its own rich gravy. Letting it cool helps in the removal of any fat and improves the flavor.

Serves 5–6
1–2 tablespoons oil
5½-pound chicken
2 tablespoons all-purpose flour
½ teaspoon paprika
2½ cups boiling water
salt and freshly ground black pepper
cooked rice and broccoli, to serve

1 Preheat the oven to 325°F. Heat the oil in a large, flameproof casserole and sauté the chicken slowly on all sides until the skin is brown. A boiling fowl is fatter, so you should prick the skin with a fork on the back and legs to release the fat as the chicken cooks.

2 Transfer the chicken to a plate and sprinkle the flour on the oil remaining in the casserole, adding a little more if necessary, to make a paste. Add the paprika and seasoning, and gradually pour in the boiling water, stirring constantly to make a thick sauce. When the sauce is simmering, replace the chicken, spoon some of the sauce on top and cover tightly with a sheet of aluminum foil and then the lid.

3 Cook in the center of the oven for about 1 hour and then turn the chicken over. Continue cooking for about 2 hours or until the chicken is tender (a roaster will cook much quicker than a boiler). Add a little extra boiling water if the sauce appears to be drying up.

4 When the meat on the legs is tender, the chicken is done. Let cool, then pour the gravy into a bowl. When it is cold, chill in the refrigerator until the fat solidifies into a pale layer on top. Remove with a spoon.

5 Joint the chicken, place in a clean pan and pour in the cold gravy. Reheat thoroughly and serve with rice and broccoli.

Pan-fried Chicken with Pesto

Pan-fried chicken, served with warm pesto, makes a deliciously quick main course. Serve with rice noodles and braised mixed vegetables.

Serves 4
1 tablespoon olive oil
4 chicken breast fillets, skinned
fresh basil leaves, to garnish
braised baby carrots and celery, to serve

For the pesto
6 tablespoons olive oil
½ cup pine nuts
⅔ cup grated Parmesan cheese
1 cup fresh basil leaves
¼ cup fresh parsley
2 garlic cloves, crushed
salt and freshly ground black pepper

1 Heat the 1 tablespoon oil in a frying pan. Add the chicken fillets and cook gently for 15–20 minutes, turning several times, until tender, lightly browned and thoroughly cooked.

2 Meanwhile, to make the pesto, place the olive oil, pine nuts, Parmesan cheese, basil, parsley, garlic and salt and pepper to taste in a blender or food processor, and process until smooth and well mixed.

3 Remove the chicken from the pan, cover and keep hot. Reduce the heat slightly, then add the pesto to the pan and cook gently, stirring constantly, for a few minutes until the pesto has warmed through.

4 Pour the warm pesto over the chicken, then garnish with basil leaves and serve with braised baby carrots and celery.

Succulent Fried Chicken

Crisp-coated deep-fried chicken, tender and succulent within, is justifiably popular.

Serves 4
1 cup milk
1 egg, beaten
1¼ cups all-purpose flour
1 teaspoon paprika
8 chicken portions
oil, for deep-frying
salt and freshly ground black pepper
lemon wedges and fresh flat-leaf parsley, to garnish

1 Mix the milk with the beaten egg in a shallow dish. On a sheet of waxed paper, combine the flour, paprika, salt and pepper.

2 One at a time, dip the chicken portions in the egg mixture and turn them to coat all over. Then dip them in the flour and shake off any excess.

3 Deep-fry in hot oil for 25–30 minutes, turning the pieces so they brown and cook evenly. Drain well on paper towels and serve very hot, garnished with lemon wedges and parsley.

Chicken Bitki

A Polish dish, in which finely chopped chicken and mushrooms are formed into small sausage shapes and fried. You could use guinea fowl to mimic the flavor of Polish chicken.

Makes 12
1 tablespoon butter, melted
1½ cups flat mushrooms, finely chopped
1 cup fresh white bread crumbs
12 ounces chicken breast fillet, skinned and finely chopped
2 eggs, separated
¼ teaspoon grated nutmeg
2 tablespoons all-purpose flour
3 tablespoons oil
salt and freshly ground black pepper
green salad and grated pickled beets, to serve

1 Melt the butter in a pan and cook the mushrooms for 5 minutes, until they are soft and all the juices have evaporated. Set aside to cool.

2 Combine the bread crumbs, chicken, egg yolks, nutmeg, salt and pepper and mushrooms in a bowl.

3 In a clean bowl, whisk the egg whites until stiff. Stir half into the chicken mixture, then fold in the remainder.

4 Shape the mixture into 12 even sausages, about 3 inches long and 1 inch wide. Roll in the flour to coat.

5 Heat the oil in a frying pan and fry the bitki for 10 minutes, turning until evenly golden brown and cooked through. Serve hot with a green salad and pickled beets.

Cook's Tip
It is always better to use freshly grated nutmeg rather than ready ground because the essential oils that give it its flavor are very volatile.

Layered Chicken & Mushroom Potato Casserole

A delicious and moist combination of chicken, vegetables and gravy in a simple, one-dish meal topped with crunchy slices of potato.

Serves 4–6
1 tablespoon olive oil
4 large chicken breast fillets, cut into chunks
1 leek, finely sliced into rings
¼ cup butter
¼ cup all-purpose flour
2 cups milk
1 teaspoon whole-grain mustard
1 carrot, very finely diced
3 cups button mushrooms, finely sliced
2 pounds potatoes, finely sliced
salt and freshly ground black pepper

1 Preheat the oven to 350°F. Heat the oil in a large saucepan and cook the chicken for 5 minutes, until browned. Add the leek and sauté for another 5 minutes.

2 Add half the butter to the pan and let it melt. Then sprinkle on the flour and stir in the milk. Cook over low heat until thickened, then stir in the mustard. Add the carrots with the mushrooms. Season with salt and pepper.

3 Line the bottom of a 7½-cup ovenproof dish with potato slices. Spoon on one third of the chicken mixture. Cover with another layer of potatoes. Repeat the layering, finishing with a layer of potatoes. Top with the remaining butter.

4 Bake for 1½ hours, covering with aluminum foil after 30 minutes' cooking time. Serve hot.

> **Cook's Tip**
> *The liquid from the mushrooms keeps the chicken moist, and the potatoes help to mop up any excess juices.*

Chicken with Potato Dumplings

Poached chicken breasts in a creamy sauce topped with light herb and potato dumplings make a delicate yet hearty meal.

Serves 6
1 onion, chopped
1¼ cups vegetable stock
½ cup white wine
4 large chicken breasts
1¼ cups light cream
1 tablespoon chopped fresh tarragon
salt and freshly ground black pepper

For the dumplings
8 ounces potatoes, boiled and mashed
1¼ cups suet
1 cup self-rising flour
2 tablespoons chopped mixed fresh herbs
¼ cup water

1 Place the onion, stock and wine in a deep-sided frying pan. Add the chicken and simmer for 20 minutes, covered. Remove the chicken from the stock, cut into chunks and reserve.

2 Strain the stock and discard the onion. Reduce the stock by one third over high heat. Stir in the cream and tarragon, and simmer until just thickened. Stir in the chicken and season. Spoon the mixture into a 3¾-cup ovenproof dish. Preheat the oven to 375°F.

3 To make the dumplings, combine the ingredients in a bowl with salt and pepper, and stir in the water to make a soft dough. Divide into six and shape into balls with floured hands.

4 Place on top of the chicken mixture and bake uncovered for 30 minutes, until the dumplings are browned and cooked through. Serve immediately.

> **Cook's Tip**
> *Do not reduce the sauce too much before it is cooked in the oven, as the dumplings absorb quite a lot of the liquid.*

Persian Chicken

A sauce flavored with cinnamon, saffron and lemon juice makes this simple dish quite special.

Serves 4
1 tablespoon oil
4 chicken portions
1 large onion, chopped
3 garlic cloves, finely chopped
1 teaspoon ground cinnamon
2–3 saffron threads, soaked in 1 tablespoon boiling water
2 tablespoons lemon juice
2 cups water
salt and freshly ground black pepper
cooked rice, yogurt and salad, to serve

1 Heat the oil in a large saucepan or flameproof casserole and sauté the chicken portions until golden. Remove from the pan and set aside.

2 Add the onion to the pan and sauté gently over medium heat for about 5 minutes, stirring frequently, until softened and golden, then add the garlic and cook briefly.

3 Stir in the cinnamon, saffron, lemon juice and seasoning. Return the chicken to the pan, add the water and bring to a boil over medium heat.

4 Reduce the heat, cover and simmer for 30–45 minutes until the chicken is cooked and the sauce is reduced to ½ cup. Serve with rice, yogurt and salad.

> **Cook's Tip**
> *Cinnamon is the dried rolled bark of a tropical tree. It is available in sticks, which are difficult to grind, and ready ground.*

Chicken with Cajun Sauce

Real Cajun sauce must start with a Cajun roux.

Serves 4
1 cup all-purpose flour
3½-pound chicken, cut into 8 portions
1 cup buttermilk
vegetable oil, for frying
salt and freshly ground black pepper
fresh parsley sprigs, to garnish

For the sauce
½ cup lard or vegetable oil
generous ½ cup all-purpose flour
2 onions, chopped
2–3 celery stalks, chopped
1 large green bell pepper, seeded and chopped
2 garlic cloves, finely chopped
1 cup passata
scant 2 cups red wine or Chicken Stock
8 ounces tomatoes, peeled and chopped
2 bay leaves
1 tablespoon brown sugar
1 teaspoon grated orange zest
½ teaspoon cayenne pepper

1 To make the sauce, melt the lard and stir in the flour. Cook over low heat, stirring, for 15–20 minutes or until golden brown.

2 Add the onions, celery, green pepper and garlic and cook, stirring, until softened. Stir in the remaining sauce ingredients and season. Bring to a boil, then simmer for 1 hour or until the sauce is rich and thick. Stir occasionally.

3 Meanwhile, prepare the chicken. Put the flour in a plastic bag and season. Dip each piece of chicken in buttermilk, then dredge in the flour. Set aside for 20 minutes.

4 Heat 1 inch oil in a frying pan. Fry the chicken pieces, turning once, for 30 minutes, until deep golden and cooked. Drain on paper towels. Add them to the sauce, garnish and serve.

Crunchy Stuffed Chicken Breasts

These can be prepared ahead of time as long as the stuffing is quite cold before it is spooned into the "pockets." It is an ideal dish for entertaining.

Serves 4
4 chicken breast fillets
2 tablespoons butter
1 garlic clove, crushed
1 tablespoon Dijon mustard
cooked vegetables, to serve

For the stuffing
1 tablespoon butter
1 bunch scallions, sliced
3 tablespoons fresh bread crumbs
2 tablespoons pine nuts
1 egg yolk
1 tablespoon chopped fresh parsley
salt and freshly ground black pepper
¼ cup grated cheese

For the topping
2 strips bacon, finely chopped
1 cup fresh bread crumbs
1 tablespoon grated Parmesan cheese
1 tablespoon chopped fresh parsley

1 Preheat the oven to 400°F. First, make the stuffing. Heat the butter in a heavy frying pan and cook the scallions, stirring occasionally, until soft. Remove from heat and let cool for a few minutes. Add the remaining ingredients and mix thoroughly.

2 To make the topping, fry the chopped bacon until crisp, then drain well on paper towels. Place the bread crumbs, grated Parmesan cheese and parsley in a bowl, and add the bacon. Mix thoroughly to combine.

3 Carefully cut a pocket in each chicken breast, using a sharp knife. Divide the stuffing into fourths and use to fill the pockets. Transfer the chicken breasts to a buttered ovenproof dish.

4 Melt the remaining butter, mix it with the crushed garlic and mustard, and brush liberally on the chicken. Press on the topping and bake, uncovered, for 30–40 minutes or until tender. Serve with vegetables.

Oven-fried Chicken

An easy way of cooking "fried" chicken with a crisp bread crumb coating—once it is in the oven, you can turn your attention to preparing the rest of the meal without any worries.

Serves 4
4 large chicken portions
½ cup all-purpose flour
½ teaspoon salt
¼ teaspoon black pepper
1 egg
2 tablespoons water
2 tablespoons finely chopped mixed fresh herbs, e.g. parsley, basil and thyme
1 cup fresh bread crumbs
¾ cup grated Parmesan cheese
oil, for greasing
lemon wedges, to serve

1 Preheat the oven to 400°F. Rinse the chicken portions and pat dry with paper towels.

2 Combine the flour, salt and pepper on a large plate and stir with a fork to mix. Coat the chicken portions on all sides with the seasoned flour and shake off the excess.

3 Sprinkle a little water onto the chicken portions and coat again lightly with the seasoned flour.

4 Beat the egg with 2 tablespoons water in a shallow dish and stir in the herbs. Combine the bread crumbs and grated Parmesan cheese on a plate.

5 Dip the chicken portions into the egg mixture, turning to coat them evenly, then roll in the bread crumbs, patting them on with your fingertips to help them stick.

6 Place the chicken portions in a greased shallow roasting pan or ovenproof dish large enough to hold them in one layer. Bake for 20–30 minutes until thoroughly cooked and golden brown. Serve immediately, with lemon wedges for squeezing.

Pan-fried Chicken

The essence of this dish is to cook it quickly over high heat, and it therefore works best with small amounts. To serve four people, double the amount and either cook in batches or use two pans.

Serves 2
2 chicken breast fillets, skinned
1 small fresh red or green chile, seeded and finely sliced
2 garlic cloves, finely sliced
3 scallions, sliced
4–5 thin slices fresh ginger root
½ teaspoon ground coriander
½ teaspoon ground cumin
2 tablespoons olive oil
1½ tablespoons lemon juice
2 tablespoons pine nuts
1 tablespoon raisins (optional)
oil, for frying
1 tablespoon chopped cilantro
1 tablespoon chopped fresh mint
salt and freshly ground black pepper
sprigs of fresh mint and lemon wedges, to garnish
cooked rice or couscous, to serve

1 Cut the chicken fillets lengthwise into three or four thin slices. Place in a shallow bowl. Blend together the chile, garlic, scallions, spices, olive oil, lemon juice, pine nuts and raisins, if using. Season, then pour onto the chicken pieces, stirring to coat. Cover with plastic wrap and set in a cool place for 1–2 hours.

2 Lift the chicken out of the dish, reserving the marinade. Brush a heavy frying pan with oil, and heat. Add the chicken slices and stir-fry over fairly high heat for 3–4 minutes, until the chicken is browned on all sides. Add the reserved marinade and continue to cook over high heat for 6–8 minutes, until the chicken is cooked through.

3 Reduce the heat, stir in the herbs, cook for 1 minute, then garnish and serve.

Hunter's Chicken

This traditional Italian dish sometimes has strips of green bell pepper in the sauce for extra color and flavor instead of mushrooms.

Serves 4
¼ cup dried porcini mushrooms
2 tablespoons olive oil
1 tablespoon butter
4 chicken portions, on the bone, skinned
1 large onion, thinly sliced
14-ounce can chopped tomatoes
⅔ cup red wine
1 garlic clove, crushed
leaves of 1 fresh rosemary sprig, finely chopped
1½ cups fresh field mushrooms, thinly sliced
salt and freshly ground black pepper
fresh rosemary sprigs, to garnish
creamed potatoes or polenta, to serve

1 Put the porcini in a bowl, add 1 cup warm water and let soak for 20–30 minutes. Remove from the liquid and squeeze the porcini over the bowl. Strain the liquid and reserve. Finely chop the porcini.

2 Heat the oil and butter in a large, flameproof casserole until foaming. Add the chicken and sauté over medium heat for 5 minutes or until golden. Drain on paper towels.

3 Add the onion and porcini to the pan. Cook gently, stirring frequently, for 3 minutes, until the onion has softened but not browned. Stir in the chopped tomatoes, wine and reserved mushroom soaking liquid, then add the crushed garlic and chopped rosemary, with salt and pepper to taste. Bring to a boil, stirring constantly.

4 Return the chicken to the casserole and turn to coat with the sauce. Cover and simmer gently for 30 minutes.

5 Add the fresh mushrooms and stir well to mix into the sauce. Continue simmering gently for 10 minutes or until the chicken is tender. Taste and adjust the seasoning as necessary. Transfer to a warmed serving dish and garnish with rosemary. Serve hot, with creamed potatoes or polenta, if desired.

Country Chicken Sauté

Chicken in a bacon, mushroom and wine sauce.

Serves 4
1 cup chopped bacon
2 teaspoons oil
3½-pound chicken, cut into 8 portions
seasoned flour, for coating
3 cups mushrooms, quartered
butter
3 tablespoons dry white wine
1 cup Chicken Stock

1 Cook the bacon in the oil until lightly colored. Remove and reserve.

2 Dredge the chicken in seasoned flour and fry until evenly browned. Remove and set aside.

3 Add the mushrooms and butter to the pan, and sauté until softened. Return the bacon and chicken, and add the wine and stock. Bring to a boil, cover and cook over low heat for 20–25 minutes or until the chicken is tender.

Mediterranean Chicken

This is the perfect after-work supper-party dish: it is quick to prepare and full of sunshiny flavors.

Serves 4

4 chicken breast portions, about 1½ pounds total weight
1 cup cream cheese with garlic and herbs
1 pound zucchini
2 red bell peppers, seeded
1 pound plum tomatoes
4 celery stalks
about 3 tablespoons olive oil
10 ounces onions, roughly chopped
3 garlic cloves, crushed
8 sun-dried tomatoes, roughly chopped
1 teaspoon dried oregano
2 tablespoons balsamic vinegar
1 teaspoon paprika
salt and freshly ground black pepper
olive ciabatta or crusty bread, to serve

1 Preheat the oven to 375°F. Loosen the skin of each chicken portion, without removing it, to make a pocket. Divide the cheese into four pieces and push one quarter underneath the skin of each chicken portion in an even layer.

2 Cut the zucchini and peppers into similar-size chunky pieces. Quarter the tomatoes and slice the celery stalks.

3 Heat 2 tablespoons of the oil in a large, shallow, flameproof casserole. Cook the onions and garlic for 4 minutes, until they are soft and golden, stirring frequently.

4 Add the zucchini, peppers and celery to the casserole, and cook for another 5 minutes.

5 Stir in the tomatoes, sun-dried tomatoes, oregano and balsamic vinegar. Season well.

6 Place the chicken on top of the vegetables, drizzle on a little more olive oil, and season with salt and the paprika. Bake for 35–40 minutes or until the chicken is golden and cooked through. Serve with plenty of olive ciabatta or crusty bread to mop up the juices.

Stuffed Chicken Breasts

This dish consists of large chicken breasts filled with an herbed spinach mixture, then topped with butter and baked until mouth-wateringly tender.

Serves 6

4 ounces potatoes, diced
4 ounces spinach leaves, finely chopped
1 egg, beaten
2 tablespoons chopped cilantro
4 large chicken breasts
¼ cup butter
salt and freshly ground black pepper
cilantro sprigs, to garnish
fried mushrooms, to serve

For the sauce
14-ounce can chopped tomatoes
1 garlic clove, crushed
⅔ cup Chicken Stock
2 tablespoons chopped cilantro

1 Preheat the oven to 350°F. Boil the potatoes in a large saucepan of boiling water for 15 minutes or until tender. Drain, place in a large bowl and roughly mash.

2 Stir the spinach into the potato with the egg and cilantro. Season with salt and pepper to taste.

3 Cut almost all the way through the chicken breasts and open out to form a pocket in each. Spoon the filling into the center and fold the chicken back over again. Secure with toothpicks and place in a roasting pan. Dot with butter and cover with aluminum foil. Bake for 25 minutes. Remove the foil and cook for another 10 minutes, until the chicken is golden.

4 Meanwhile, to make the sauce, heat the tomatoes, garlic and stock in a saucepan. Boil rapidly for 10 minutes. Season and stir in the cilantro.

5 Remove the chicken from the oven and place on warmed serving plates with fried mushrooms. Pour on the sauce, garnish with cilantro and serve.

Chicken with Olives

Chicken breast fillets may be flattened for quick and even cooking. Here they are prepared with black olives and tomatoes.

Serves 4

4 chicken breast fillets, about 5–6 ounces each, skinned
1/4 teaspoon cayenne pepper
5–7 tablespoons extra virgin olive oil
1 garlic clove, finely chopped
16–24 pitted black olives
6 ripe plum tomatoes, quartered
small handful of fresh basil leaves
salt

1 Place each chicken breast between two sheets of plastic wrap and pound with the flat side of a meat mallet or roll out with a rolling pin to flatten to about 1/2 inch thick. Season with salt and the cayenne pepper.

2 Heat 3–4 tablespoons of the olive oil in a large, heavy frying pan over medium-high heat. Add the chicken and cook for 4–5 minutes, until golden brown and just cooked, turning once. Transfer the chicken to warmed serving plates and keep warm.

3 Wipe out the frying pan and return to the heat. Add the remaining oil and sauté the garlic for 1 minute until golden and fragrant. Stir in the olives, cook for another minute, then stir in the tomatoes.

4 Shred the basil leaves and stir into the olive and tomato mixture, then spoon it over the chicken and serve immediately.

Cook's Tip
If the tomato skins are at all tough, remove them. Score the bottom of each tomato with a knife, then plunge them into boiling water for 45 seconds. Cool quickly in cold water. The skin should then peel off easily.

Chicken, Carrot & Leek Parcels

These intriguing parcels may sound a bit tricky for every-day cooking, but they take very little time to make and you can freeze them—ready to cook gently from frozen.

Serves 4

oil, for greasing
2 small leeks, sliced
4 chicken breast fillets
2 carrots, grated
4 pitted black olives, chopped
1 garlic clove, crushed
1–2 tablespoons olive oil
8 canned anchovy fillets, drained
salt and freshly ground black pepper
black olives and fresh herb sprigs, to garnish

1 Preheat the oven to 400°F. Prepare four sheets of waxed paper about 9 inches square and grease them.

2 Divide the leeks equally among the sheets of waxed paper, placing them near the edge. Season the chicken fillets well on both sides and place one on each pile of leeks.

3 Combine the carrots, olives, garlic and oil. Season lightly and place on top of the chicken portions. Top each with two of the anchovy fillets, then carefully wrap up each parcel, making sure the paper folds are secure and positioned underneath and that the carrot mixture is on top.

4 Bake for 20 minutes and serve hot, in the paper, garnished with black olives and fresh herb sprigs.

Cook's Tip
You can also wrap the chicken and vegetables in aluminum foil, but remove the foil before serving.

Duck & Ginger Chop Suey

Chicken can also be used in this recipe, but duck gives a richer contrast of flavors.

Serves 4
2 duck breasts, about 6 ounces each
3 tablespoons sunflower oil
1 small egg, lightly beaten
1 garlic clove
¾ cup bean sprouts
2 slices fresh ginger root, cut into matchsticks
2 teaspoons oyster sauce
2 scallions, cut into matchsticks
salt and freshly ground black pepper

For the marinade
1 tablespoon honey
2 teaspoons rice wine
2 teaspoons light soy sauce
2 teaspoons dark soy sauce

1 Remove the skin and fat from the duck, cut the breasts into thin strips and place in a bowl. To make the marinade, combine the ingredients in a bowl. Pour the marinade onto the duck, cover and refrigerate overnight.

2 Next day, make the omelet. Heat a small frying pan and add 1 tablespoon of the oil. When the oil is hot, pour in the egg and swirl it around into an even layer. When the omelet is cooked, remove it from the pan, let it cool, then cut into strips. Drain the duck and discard the marinade.

3 Bruise the garlic with the flat side of a knife blade. Heat a wok or large frying pan, then add 2 teaspoons of the oil. When the oil is hot, add the garlic and sauté for 30 seconds, pressing it to release the flavor. Discard. Add the bean sprouts with seasoning and stir-fry for 30 seconds. Transfer to a heated dish, draining off any liquid.

4 Heat the wok again and add the remaining oil. When the oil is hot, stir-fry the duck for 3 minutes, until cooked. Add the ginger and oyster sauce, and stir-fry for another 2 minutes. Add the bean sprouts, egg strips and scallions, stir-fry briefly and serve immediately.

Stir-fried Crispy Duck

This stir-fry would be delicious wrapped in flour tortillas or steamed Chinese pancakes, served with a little extra warm plum sauce.

Serves 2
10–12 ounce duck breast fillets
2 tablespoons all-purpose flour
¼ cup oil
1 bunch scallions, halved lengthwise and cut into 2-inch strips
2½ cups green cabbage, finely shredded
8-ounce can water chestnuts, drained and sliced
½ cup unsalted cashews
4 ounces cucumber, cut into strips
3 tablespoons plum sauce
1 tablespoon light soy sauce
salt and freshly ground black pepper
sliced scallions, to garnish

1 Trim the skin and a little of the fat off the duck and thinly slice the meat. Season the flour well and use it to coat each piece of duck.

2 Heat the oil in a wok or large frying pan and cook the duck over high heat until golden and crisp. Keep stirring to prevent the duck from sticking. Remove using a slotted spoon and drain on paper towels. You may need to cook the duck in batches.

3 Add the scallions to the pan and cook for 2 minutes. Stir in the shredded cabbage and cook for 5 minutes or until softened and golden.

4 Return the duck to the pan with the water chestnuts, cashews and cucumber. Stir-fry for 2 minutes.

5 Add the plum sauce and soy sauce with plenty of seasoning, and heat for 2 minutes. Serve piping hot, garnished with sliced scallions.

Stir-fried Turkey with Broccoli & Mushrooms

This is a really easy, tasty supper dish that works well with chicken too.

Serves 4
4 ounces broccoli florets
4 scallions
1 teaspoon cornstarch
3 tablespoons oyster sauce
1 tablespoon dark soy sauce
½ cup Chicken Stock
2 teaspoons lemon juice
3 tablespoons peanut oil
1 pound turkey steaks, cut into strips about ¼ × 2 inches
1 small onion, chopped
2 garlic cloves, crushed
2 teaspoons grated fresh ginger root
4 ounces fresh shiitake mushrooms, sliced
⅓ cup baby corn, halved lengthwise
1 tablespoon sesame oil
salt and freshly ground black pepper
egg noodles, to serve

1 Divide the broccoli florets into smaller sprigs and cut the stalks into thin diagonal slices. Finely chop the white parts of the scallions and slice the green parts into thin shreds. In a bowl, blend together the cornstarch, oyster sauce, soy sauce, stock and lemon juice. Set aside.

2 Heat a wok until hot, add 2 tablespoons of the peanut oil and swirl it around. Add the turkey and stir-fry for about 2 minutes, until golden and crispy at the edges. Remove the turkey from the wok and keep warm.

3 Add the remaining oil and stir-fry the onion, garlic and ginger for about 1 minute. Increase the heat, add the broccoli, mushrooms and corn, and stir-fry for 2 minutes.

4 Return the turkey to the wok, then add the sauce with the chopped scallion whites and seasoning. Cook, stirring, for about 1 minute, until the sauce has thickened. Stir in the sesame oil. Serve immediately on a bed of egg noodles with the finely shredded scallion greens on top.

Turkey Rolls with Gazpacho Sauce

This Spanish-style recipe uses quick-cooking turkey steaks, which are served with a refreshing sauce made from raw mixed vegetables.

Serves 4
4 turkey breast steaks
1 tablespoon red pesto or tomato paste
4 chorizo sausages

For the gazpacho sauce
1 green bell pepper, seeded and chopped
1 red bell pepper, seeded and chopped
3-inch piece cucumber
1 medium-size tomato
1 garlic clove
3 tablespoons olive oil
1 tablespoon red wine vinegar
salt and freshly ground black pepper

1 To make the gazpacho sauce, place the peppers, cucumber, tomato, garlic, 2 tablespoons of the oil and the vinegar in a food processor, and process until almost smooth. Season to taste with salt and pepper, and set aside.

2 If the turkey breast steaks are quite thick, place them between two sheets of plastic wrap and beat them with the side of a rolling pin, to flatten them slightly.

3 Spread the pesto or tomato paste on the turkey and then place a chorizo on each piece and roll up firmly.

4 Slice the rolls thickly and thread them onto skewers, piercing them through the spiral. Cook on a medium-hot grill or under a preheated broiler for 10–12 minutes, brushing with remaining oil and turning once. Serve with the gazpacho sauce.

Cook's Tip
If using wooden skewers, soak them in cold water for 30 minutes to prevent them from charring.

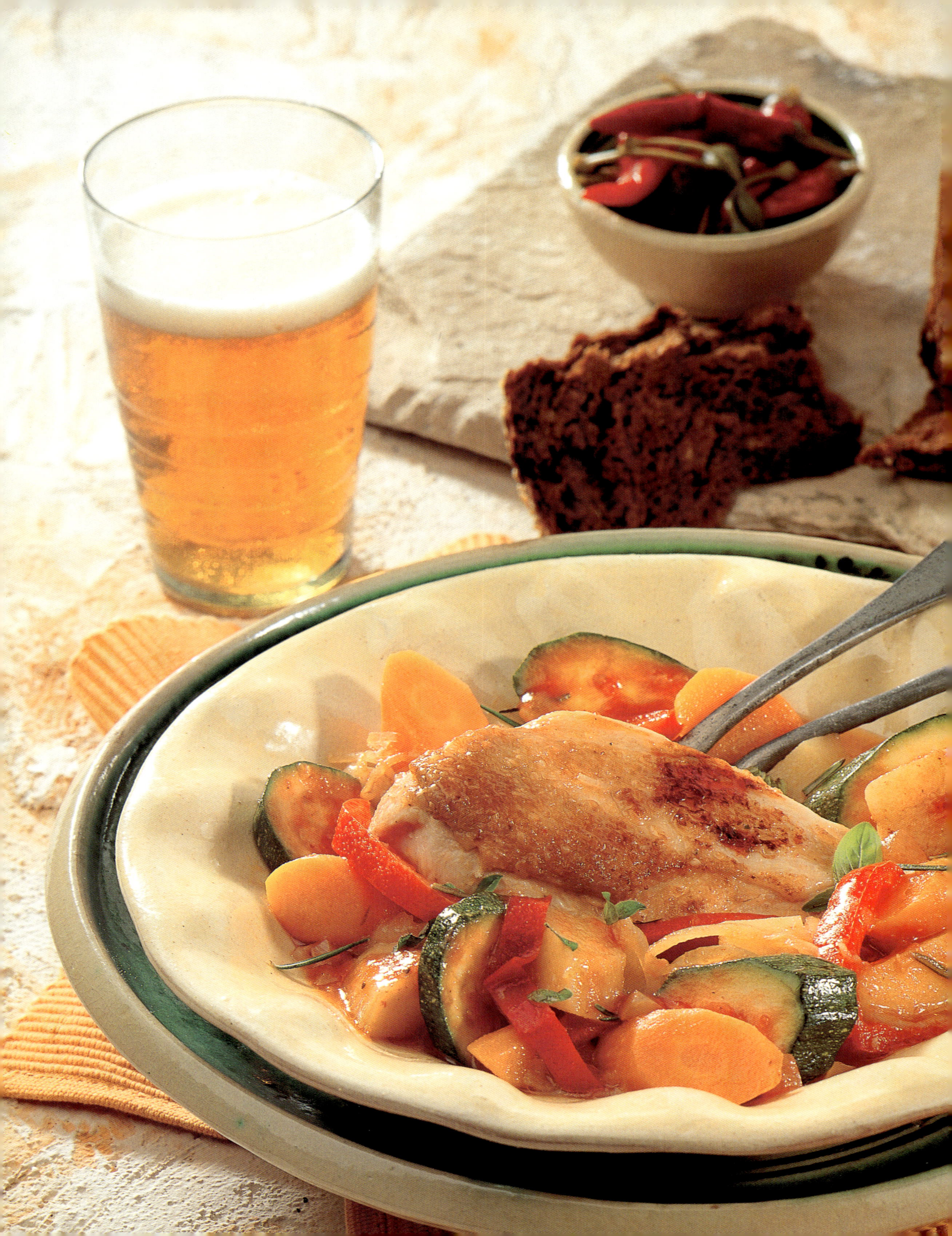

CHICKEN ROASTS, CASSEROLES & PIES

Traditional Roast Chicken

Serve with bacon rolls, chipolata sausages, gravy and stuffing balls or Bread Sauce.

Serves 4
3½-pound chicken
4 strips bacon
2 tablespoons butter
salt and freshly ground
    black pepper

For the prune and nut stuffing
2 tablespoons butter
½ cup chopped
    pitted prunes
½ cup chopped walnuts
1 cup fresh bread crumbs
1 egg, beaten
1 tablespoon chopped
    fresh parsley
1 tablespoon snipped fresh chives
2 tablespoons sherry or port

For the gravy
2 tablespoons all-purpose flour
1¼ cups Chicken Stock or
    vegetable cooking water

1 Preheat the oven to 375°F. To make the stuffing, combine all the ingredients in a bowl and season well. Stuff the neck end of the chicken quite loosely, allowing room for the bread crumbs to swell during cooking. (Any remaining stuffing can be shaped into small balls and fried.) Tuck the neck skin under the bird to secure the stuffing and hold in place with the wing tips or sew with thread or fine strips.

2 Place in a roasting pan and cover with the bacon. Spread with the butter, cover loosely with aluminum foil and roast for about 1½ hours, until the juices run clear when the thickest part of the thigh is pierced with a knife or skewer. Baste with the juices in the roasting pan three or four times during cooking.

3 Remove any trussing string and transfer to a serving plate. Cover with the foil and let rest while making the gravy. Carefully spoon off the fat from the juices in the roasting pan. Blend the flour into the juices and cook gently until golden brown. Add the stock or vegetable water and bring to a boil, stirring until thickened. Adjust the seasoning to taste, then strain the gravy into a pitcher or gravy boat. Serve with the chicken.

Honey Roast Chicken

A delicious variation on the classic roast chicken, this is filled with a bacon and mushroom stuffing and basted with honey and brandy.

Serves 4
3½-pound chicken
2 tablespoons honey
1 tablespoon brandy
5 teaspoons all-purpose flour
⅔ cup Chicken Stock
green beans, to serve

For the stuffing
2 shallots, chopped
4 strips bacon, chopped
¾ cup button mushrooms,
    quartered
1 tablespoon butter
    or margarine
2 thick slices white bread, diced
1 tablespoon chopped
    fresh parsley
salt and freshly ground
    black pepper

1 To make the stuffing, gently fry the shallots, bacon and mushrooms in a frying pan for 5 minutes, then transfer to a bowl. Pour off all but 2 tablespoons of bacon fat from the pan. Add the butter or margarine to the pan and fry the bread until golden brown. Add the bread to the bacon mixture. Stir in the parsley, and salt and pepper to taste. Let cool.

2 Preheat the oven to 350°F. Pack the stuffing into the neck end of the chicken and truss with string. Transfer the chicken to a roasting pan that just holds it.

3 Mix the honey with the brandy. Brush half of the mixture over the chicken. Roast for about 1 hour and 20 minutes, until the juices run clear when the thickest part of the thigh is pierced with a skewer or knife. Baste the chicken frequently with the remaining honey mixture during roasting.

4 Transfer the chicken to a warmed serving platter. Cover with aluminum foil and set aside. Strain the cooking juices into a degreasing pitcher. Set aside to let the fat rise, then pour off the fat. Stir the flour into the sediment in the roasting pan. Add the cooking juices and the chicken stock. Boil rapidly until the gravy has thickened, stirring constantly to prevent lumps from forming. Pour into a gravy boat and serve with the chicken and green beans.

Roast Chicken with Fresh Herbs & Garlic

A smaller chicken can also be roasted in this way.

Serves 4

4-pound chicken or
   4 small poussins
finely grated zest and juice of
   1 lemon
1 garlic clove, crushed
2 tablespoons olive oil
2 fresh thyme sprigs
2 fresh sage sprigs
6 tablespoons unsalted
   butter, softened
salt and freshly ground
   black pepper

1 Season the chicken or poussins well with salt and pepper. Combine the lemon zest and juice, garlic and olive oil and pour over the chicken. Let marinate for at least 2 hours in a nonmetallic dish.

2 When the chicken has marinated, preheat the oven to 450°F. Place the herbs in the cavity of the bird and smear the butter on the skin. Season well.

3 Roast the chicken for 10 minutes, then turn the oven down to 375°F. Baste the chicken well and then roast for another 1½ hours, until the juices run clear when the thickest part of the thigh is pierced with a skewer or knife. Let rest for 10–15 minutes before carving to serve.

Bread Sauce

Smooth and surprisingly delicate, this old-fashioned sauce is traditionally served with roast chicken, turkey and various game birds.

Serves 6

1 small onion
4 cloves
1 bay leaf
1¼ cups milk
2 cups fresh
   white bread crumbs
1 tablespoon butter
1 tablespoon light cream
salt and freshly ground
   black pepper

1 Peel the onion and stick the cloves into it. Put it into a saucepan with the bay leaf and milk. Bring to a boil, then remove from heat and set aside for 15–20 minutes.

2 Remove the bay leaf and onion. Return to the heat and stir in the bread crumbs. Simmer for 4–5 minutes or until thick and creamy. Stir in the butter and cream, then season to taste.

Roast Chicken with Lemon & Herbs

For this French roasting method, a well-flavored chicken is essential—use a free-range or corn-fed bird if possible.

Serves 4

3-pound chicken
1 unwaxed lemon, halved
small bunch of fresh thyme sprigs
1 bay leaf
1 tablespoon butter, softened
4–6 tablespoons Chicken Stock
   or water
salt and freshly ground
   black pepper

1 Preheat the oven to 400°F. Season the chicken inside and out with salt and pepper.

2 Squeeze the juice of one lemon half and then place the juice, the squeezed lemon half, the thyme and bay leaf in the chicken cavity. Tie the legs with string and rub the breast with butter.

3 Place the chicken on a rack in a roasting pan. Squeeze on the juice of the other lemon half. Roast the chicken for 1 hour, basting two or three times, until the juices run clear when the thickest part of the thigh is pierced with a knife or skewer.

4 Pour the juices from the cavity into the roasting pan and transfer the chicken to a carving board. Cover loosely with aluminum foil and let rest for 10–15 minutes before carving.

5 Skim off the fat from the cooking juices. Add the stock or water and boil over medium heat, scraping the bottom of the pan, until slightly reduced. Strain and serve with the chicken.

> **Cook's Tip**
> Be sure to save the carcasses of roast poultry for stock. Freeze them until you have several, then simmer with aromatic vegetables, herbs and water.

Crispy Roast Spring Chickens

These small birds, roasted with a honey glaze, are delicious either hot or cold. One bird is sufficient for two servings.

Serves 4
2 2-pound chickens
2 tablespoons honey
2 tablespoons sherry
1 tablespoon vinegar
salt and freshly ground
   black pepper
salad greens and lime wedges,
   to garnish

1 Preheat the oven to 350°F. Tie the birds into shape and place on a wire rack over the sink. Pour on boiling water to plump the flesh, then pat dry with paper towels.

2 To make the honey glaze, combine the honey, sherry and vinegar together in a small bowl, and brush over the birds. Season well.

3 Place the rack in a roasting pan and cook for 45–55 minutes, basting with the glaze until crisp and golden brown. Garnish with salad greens and lime wedges, and serve hot or cold.

Basic Herb Stuffing

This simple herb stuffing is suitable for all poultry.

1 small onion, finely chopped
1 tablespoon butter
2 cups fresh
   white bread crumbs
1 tablespoon chopped
   fresh parsley
1 teaspoon dried mixed herbs
1 egg, beaten
salt and freshly ground
   black pepper

1 Sauté the onion in the butter until tender. Set aside to cool.
2 Add to the remaining ingredients and mix thoroughly. Season well with salt and pepper.

Middle Eastern Spring Chickens

This dish is widely enjoyed in Lebanon and Syria. The stuffing is a delicious blend of meat, nuts and rice.

Serves 6–8
2 2¼-pound chickens
about 1 tablespoon butter
plain yogurt and salad, to serve

For the stuffing
3 tablespoons oil
1 onion, chopped
1 pound ground lamb
¾ cup almonds, chopped
¾ cup pine nuts
1½ cups cooked rice
salt and freshly ground
   black pepper

1 Preheat the oven to 350°F. To make the stuffing, heat the oil in a large frying pan and sauté the onion over low heat until slightly softened. Add the ground lamb and cook over medium heat for 4–8 minutes, until well browned, stirring frequently. Set aside.

2 Heat a small, heavy pan over medium heat and dry-fry the almonds and pine nuts for 2–3 minutes, until golden, shaking the pan frequently.

3 Combine the meat mixture, almonds, pine nuts and cooked rice. Season to taste with salt and pepper. Spoon the stuffing mixture into the body cavities of the chickens. (Cook any leftover stuffing separately in a greased ovenproof dish.) Rub the chickens all over with the butter.

4 Place the chickens in a large roasting pan, cover with aluminum foil and bake for 45–60 minutes. After about 30 minutes, remove the foil and baste the chickens with the cooking juices.

5 Continue roasting without the foil until the chickens are cooked through: the juices will run clear when the thickest part of the thigh is pierced with a skewer or knife. Serve the chickens, cut into portions, with yogurt and a salad.

French-style Pot-roast Poussins

Small, young chickens are cooked with tender baby vegetables in a wine-enriched stock—the perfect early summer meal.

Serves 4

1 tablespoon olive oil
1 onion, sliced
1 large garlic clove, sliced
⅓ cup diced bacon
2 poussins, just under 1 pound each
2 tablespoons melted butter
2 baby celery hearts, quartered
8 baby carrots
2 small zucchini, cut into chunks
8 small new potatoes
2½ cups Chicken Stock
⅔ cup dry white wine
1 bay leaf
2 fresh thyme sprigs
2 fresh rosemary sprigs
1 tablespoon butter, softened
1 tablespoon all-purpose flour
salt and freshly ground black pepper
fresh herbs, to garnish

1 Preheat the oven to 375°F. Heat the oil in a large, flameproof casserole and add the onion, garlic and bacon. Sauté for 5–6 minutes, until the onions have softened. Brush the poussins with a little of the melted butter and season well. Place on top of the onion mixture and arrange the prepared vegetables around them. Pour the chicken stock and wine around the birds, and add the herbs.

2 Cover, cook for 20 minutes, then remove the lid and brush the birds with the remaining melted butter. Cook for another 25–30 minutes, until golden.

3 Transfer the poussins to a warmed serving platter and cut each in half. Remove the vegetables with a draining spoon and arrange them around the birds. Cover with aluminum foil and keep warm.

4 Discard the herbs from the cooking juices. In a bowl, mix the softened butter and flour to form a paste. Bring the cooking liquid to a boil and then whisk in spoonfuls of the paste until thickened. Season the sauce, and serve with the poussins and vegetables, garnished with herbs.

Baby Chickens with Cranberry Sauce

Fresh cranberries make a delicious sauce for these simply roasted poussins.

Serves 4

4 poussins, with giblets (optional), about 1 pound each
3 tablespoons butter or margarine
1 onion, quartered
¼ cup port
¾ cup Chicken Stock
2 tablespoons honey
1¼ cups cranberries
salt and freshly ground black pepper
cooked new potatoes and broccoli, to serve

1 Preheat the oven to 450°F. Smear the poussins on all sides with 2 tablespoons of the butter or margarine. Arrange them, on their sides, in a roasting pan in which they will fit comfortably. Sprinkle them with salt and pepper. Add the onion quarters to the pan. Chop the giblets and livers, if using, and arrange them around the poussins.

2 Roast for 20 minutes, basting frequently. Turn the poussins onto their other sides and roast for 20 more minutes, basting often. Turn them breast up and continue roasting for about 15 minutes, until they are cooked through. Transfer to a warmed serving dish. Cover with aluminum foil and set aside.

3 Skim any fat off the juices in the roasting pan. Put the pan over medium heat and bring the juices to a boil. Add the port and bring back to a boil, stirring well to dislodge any particles sticking to the bottom of the pan.

4 Strain the sauce into a small saucepan. Add the chicken stock, return to a boil and boil until reduced by half. Stir in the honey and cranberries. Simmer for about 3 minutes, until the cranberries pop.

5 Remove the pan from heat and swirl in the remaining butter or margarine. Season to taste, pour the sauce into a pitcher or gravy boat and serve with the poussins, accompanied by new potatoes and broccoli.

Chicken, Barley & Apple Casserole

Barley is underrated as a casserole ingredient these days: it is nutritious and makes a really tasty and filling meal.

Serves 4
1 tablespoon sunflower oil
1 large onion, sliced
1 garlic clove, crushed
3 carrots, cut into sticks
2 celery stalks, thickly sliced
⅔ cup pearl barley
4 chicken breast fillets, skinned
3 cups Chicken Stock
1 bay leaf
few sprigs each of fresh thyme and marjoram, plus extra to garnish
3 apples

1 Heat the oil in a flameproof casserole and sauté the onion for about 5 minutes, until soft. Stir in the garlic, carrots and celery, and continue to cook over low heat for another 5 minutes.

2 Stir in the pearl barley, then add the chicken breast fillets, stock and herbs. Bring to a boil, lower the heat, cover the casserole and cook gently for 1 hour.

3 Core the apples and slice them thickly. Add to the casserole, replace the lid and cook for 15 more minutes or until the apples are just tender but not mushy.

4 Divide the barley, vegetables and cooking juices among four warmed plates and arrange the chicken on top. Garnish with fresh herbs and serve.

> **Cook's Tip**
> *You can also cook the casserole in a preheated 375°F oven. The timing is the same. Chicken thighs can be substituted for breast fillets—they are not as "meaty" but are a good value for the money.*

Country Cider Casserole

Root vegetables, chopped bacon and prunes all bring flavor to the wonderful cider gravy in this filling chicken dish.

Serves 4
2 tablespoons all-purpose flour
4 boneless chicken breasts
2 tablespoons butter
1 tablespoon vegetable oil
15 baby onions
4 strips bacon, chopped
2 teaspoons Dijon mustard
scant 2 cups dry cider
3 carrots, chopped
2 parsnips, chopped
12 prunes, pitted
1 fresh rosemary sprig
1 bay leaf
salt and freshly ground black pepper
mashed potatoes, to serve

1 Preheat the oven to 325°F. Place the flour and seasoning in a plastic bag, add the chicken and shake until coated. Set aside.

2 Heat the butter and oil in a flameproof casserole. Add the onions and bacon, and fry over medium heat for 4 minutes, until the onions have softened. Remove from the pan with a slotted spoon and set aside.

3 Add the floured chicken breasts to the oil in the casserole and fry until they are browned all over, then spread a little of the mustard on top of each breast.

4 Return the onions and bacon to the casserole. Pour in the cider and add the carrots, parsnips, prunes, rosemary and bay leaf. Season well. Bring to a boil, then cover and transfer to the oven. Cook for about 1½ hours, until the chicken is tender.

5 Remove the rosemary sprig and bay leaf, and serve the chicken hot with creamy mashed potatoes.

Chicken in Creamed Horseradish

The piquant flavor of the horseradish sauce gives this quick dish a sophisticated and unusual taste. If you are using fresh horseradish, halve the amount.

Serves 4
2 tablespoons olive oil
4 chicken portions
2 tablespoons butter
2 tablespoons all-purpose flour
scant 2 cups Chicken Stock
2 tablespoons horseradish sauce
1 tablespoon chopped fresh parsley
salt and freshly ground black pepper
mashed potatoes and lightly cooked green beans, to serve

1 Heat the oil in a large, flameproof casserole and gently brown the chicken portions on both sides over medium heat. Remove the chicken from the casserole and keep warm.

2 Wipe out the casserole, then add the butter and let it melt. Stir in the flour and gradually blend in the stock. Bring to a boil, stirring constantly.

3 Add the horseradish sauce and season with salt and pepper. Return the chicken to the casserole, cover and simmer for 30–40 minutes or until tender.

4 Transfer to a serving dish and sprinkle with the chopped parsley. Serve with mashed potatoes and green beans.

> **Cook's Tip**
> *Fresh horseradish requires very careful handling, as the volatile mustard oils given off when it is peeled and grated irritate the mucous membranes and the eyes, causing them to water. Dried flaked horseradish root is a safer substitute.*

Chicken with Tomatoes & Honey

An easy-to-make Moroccan-style dish served with a sprinkling of toasted almonds and sesame seeds.

Serves 4
2 tablespoons sunflower oil
2 tablespoons butter
4 chicken quarters or 1 whole chicken, quartered
1 onion, grated or very finely chopped
1 garlic clove, crushed
1 teaspoon ground cinnamon
good pinch of ground ginger
3½ pounds tomatoes, peeled, seeded and roughly chopped
2 tablespoons honey
½ cup blanched almonds
1 tablespoon sesame seeds
salt and freshly ground black pepper
corn bread, to serve

1 Heat the oil and butter in a large, flameproof casserole. Add the chicken pieces and cook over medium heat for about 3 minutes, until the chicken is lightly browned.

2 Add the onion, garlic, cinnamon, ginger, tomatoes and seasoning. Heat gently until the tomatoes begin to bubble.

3 Lower the heat, cover and simmer very gently for 1 hour, stirring and turning the chicken occasionally, until it is completely cooked through. Transfer the chicken pieces to a plate and set aside.

4 Increase the heat and cook the tomatoes until the sauce is reduced to a thick purée, stirring frequently. Stir in the honey, cook for a minute, then return the chicken to the pan and cook for 2–3 minutes to heat through. Dry-fry the almonds and sesame seeds or toast under the broiler until golden.

5 Transfer the chicken and sauce to a warmed serving dish, and sprinkle with the almonds and sesame seeds. Serve with corn bread.

Chicken, Pepper & Bean Stew

This colorful and filling one-pot meal needs only crusty bread to serve.

Serves 4–6

4-pound chicken, cut into portions
paprika
2 tablespoons olive oil
2 tablespoons butter
2 onions, chopped
½ each green and yellow bell pepper, seeded and chopped
2 cups peeled, chopped, fresh or canned plum tomatoes
1 cup white wine
2 cups Chicken Stock or water
3 tablespoons chopped fresh parsley
½ teaspoon Tabasco sauce
1 tablespoon Worcestershire sauce
2 7-ounce cans corn
4 ounces fava beans (fresh or frozen)
3 tablespoons all-purpose flour
salt and freshly ground black pepper
fresh parsley sprigs, to garnish

1 Rinse the chicken and pat dry. Sprinkle lightly with salt and a little paprika. Heat the oil with the butter in a flameproof casserole over medium-high heat. Add the chicken pieces and fry until golden brown on all sides (cook in batches, if necessary). Remove from the pan and set aside.

2 Reduce the heat and cook the onions and peppers for 8–10 minutes, until softened. Increase the heat, then add the tomatoes and their juice, the wine, stock or water, parsley, Tabasco and Worcestershire sauces. Stir and bring to a boil.

3 Return the chicken to the pan, pushing it into the sauce. Cover and simmer for 30 minutes, stirring occasionally. Stir in the corn and beans, partly cover and cook for 30 minutes.

4 Tilt the pan and skim off the surface fat. Mix the flour with a little water in a small bowl to make a paste. Stir in about ¾ cup of the hot sauce from the pan into the flour mixture and then stir into the stew and mix well. Cook for 5–8 more minutes, stirring occasionally. Taste the stew and adjust the seasoning as necessary. Serve in shallow soup dishes or large bowls, garnished with parsley sprigs.

Chicken & Eggplant Khoresh

This Persian dish is often served on festive occasions in its country of origin and is believed to have been a favorite of kings.

Serves 4

about 4 tablespoons oil
1 whole chicken or 4 large chicken portions
1 large onion, chopped
2 garlic cloves, crushed
14-ounce can chopped tomatoes
1 cup water
3 eggplant, sliced
3 bell peppers, preferably red, green and yellow, seeded and sliced
2 tablespoons lemon juice
1 tablespoon ground cinnamon
salt and freshly ground black pepper
cooked rice, to serve

1 Heat 1 tablespoon of the oil in a large saucepan or flameproof casserole and fry the chicken or chicken portions for about 10 minutes, turning to brown on all sides. Add the onion and cook for another 4–5 minutes, until the onion is golden brown.

2 Add the garlic, the chopped tomatoes and their liquid, water and seasoning. Bring to a boil, then reduce the heat, cover the pan and simmer gently for 10 minutes.

3 Meanwhile, heat the remaining oil and cook the eggplant, in batches, until lightly golden. Transfer to a plate with a slotted spoon. Add the peppers to the pan and cook for a few minutes, until slightly softened.

4 Place the eggplant on the chicken or chicken portions and then add the peppers. Sprinkle on the lemon juice and cinnamon, then cover and continue cooking over low heat for about 45 minutes or until the chicken is cooked (the juices should run clear when the thickest part of the thigh is pierced with a skewer or knife).

5 Transfer the chicken to a serving plate, and spoon the eggplant and peppers around the edge. Reheat the sauce if necessary, adjust the seasoning and pour onto the chicken. Serve with rice.

Chicken Thighs with Lemon & Garlic

Versions of this classic dish can be found in Spain and Italy, although this particular recipe is of French origin.

Serves 4

2½ cups Chicken Stock
20 large garlic cloves
2 tablespoons butter
1 tablespoon olive oil
8 chicken thighs
1 lemon, peeled, pith removed and thinly sliced
2 tablespoons all-purpose flour
⅔ cup dry white wine
salt and freshly ground black pepper
chopped fresh parsley or basil, to garnish
boiled new potatoes or rice, to serve

1 Put the stock into a pan and bring to a boil. Add the garlic cloves, cover and simmer gently for 40 minutes. Strain the stock, reserving the garlic, and set aside.

2 Heat the butter and oil in a sauté or frying pan, add the chicken thighs and cook gently on all sides until golden. Transfer them to an ovenproof dish. Preheat the oven to 375°F.

3 Distribute the reserved garlic and the lemon slices among the chicken pieces. Add the flour to the fat in the pan in which the chicken was browned and cook, stirring, for 1 minute. Add the wine, stirring constantly and scraping the bottom of the pan, then add the stock. Cook, stirring, until the sauce has thickened and is smooth. Season with salt and pepper to taste.

4 Pour the sauce on the chicken, cover and cook for 40–45 minutes. If a thicker sauce is needed, lift out the chicken pieces and reduce the sauce by boiling it rapidly until it reaches the desired consistency.

5 Sprinkle the chopped parsley or basil on the chicken and serve with boiled new potatoes or rice.

Mediterranean Chicken with Turnips

Turnips are popular in all parts of the Mediterranean, and teamed with poultry in a casserole they make a substantial meal.

Serves 4

2 tablespoons sunflower oil
8 chicken thighs or 4 chicken portions
4 small turnips
2 onions, chopped
2 garlic cloves, crushed
6 tomatoes, peeled and chopped
1 cup tomato juice
1 cup Chicken Stock
½ cup white wine
1 teaspoon paprika
good pinch of cayenne pepper
20 black olives, pitted
½ lemon, cut into wedges
salt and freshly ground black pepper
couscous, to serve

1 Preheat the oven to 325°F. Heat 1 tablespoon of the oil in a large frying pan and fry the chicken until lightly browned. Peel the turnips and cut into julienne strips.

2 Transfer the chicken to a large casserole. Add the remaining oil to the frying pan and sauté the onions and garlic for 4–5 minutes, until lightly golden brown, stirring occasionally.

3 Add the turnips and stir-fry for 2–3 minutes. Add the tomatoes, tomato juice, stock, wine, paprika, cayenne and seasoning. Bring to a boil. Pour onto the chicken. Stir in the olives and lemon wedges.

4 Cover tightly and cook for 1–1¼ hours, until the chicken is tender. Adjust the seasoning to taste. Serve on a bed of couscous.

> **Cook's Tip**
> *This dish is especially tasty made with French turnips, which have a very delicate flavor. Young turnips do not require peeling, and their pale purple and white skins will enhance the appearance of the dish.*

Individual Noodle Casseroles

Traditionally, in Japan, these individual chicken, leek and spinach casseroles are cooked in earthenware pots.

Serves 4

4 ounces boneless chicken thigh
½ teaspoon salt
½ teaspoon sake or dry white wine
½ teaspoon soy sauce
1 leek
4 ounces spinach, trimmed
11 ounces dried udon noodles or 1¼ pounds fresh noodles
4 shiitake mushrooms, stems removed
4 small eggs
seven-flavor spice, to serve

For the soup
6 cups instant dashi
4½ teaspoons soy sauce
1 teaspoon salt
1 tablespoon mirin

1 Cut the chicken into small chunks and sprinkle with the salt, sake or wine and soy sauce. Cut the leek diagonally into 1¾-inch slices. Cook the spinach in a little water for 1–2 minutes, then drain and soak in cold water for 1 minute. Drain, squeeze lightly, then cut into 1½-inch lengths.

2 Cook the noodles. Boil dried udon noodles according to the package instructions, allowing 3 minutes less than the suggested cooking time. If using fresh udon noodles, place them in boiling water, disentangle them and then drain.

3 Bring the ingredients for the soup to a boil in a saucepan "and add the chicken and leek. Skim, then cook for 5 minutes. Divide the udon noodles among four individual flameproof casseroles. Divide the soup, chicken and leeks among them. Place over medium heat, then divide the shiitake mushrooms among the casseroles.

4 Gently break an egg into each casserole. Cover and simmer for 2 minutes. Divide the spinach among the casseroles and simmer for 1 minute.

5 Serve immediately, standing the hot casseroles on plates or table mats. Sprinkle seven-flavor spice on the casseroles.

Filipino Chicken Pot

This nourishing dish is one of many taken to the Philippines by the Spanish in the 16th century.

Serves 4–6

3 chicken legs
1 tablespoon vegetable oil
12 ounces lean pork, diced
1 small carrot, roughly chopped
1 medium onion, roughly chopped
1 cup dried navy beans, soaked in water overnight
7½ cups water
1 garlic clove, crushed
2 tablespoons tomato paste
1 bay leaf
2 chicken bouillon cubes
12 ounces sweet potatoes or new potatoes, peeled
2 teaspoons chili sauce
2 tablespoons white wine vinegar
3 firm tomatoes, peeled, seeded and chopped
8 ounces Chinese cabbage, shredded
salt and freshly ground black pepper
3 scallions, shredded, to garnish
boiled rice, to serve

1 Divide the chicken drumsticks from the thighs. Chop off the narrow end of each drumstick and discard.

2 Heat the oil in a wok or large saucepan, add the chicken, pork, carrot and onion, then brown evenly.

3 Drain and rinse the navy beans; drain again. Add to the chicken with the water, garlic, tomato paste and bay leaf. Bring to a boil and simmer for 2 hours.

4 Crumble in the chicken bouillon cubes, add the sweet or new potatoes and the chili sauce, then simmer for 15–20 minutes, until the potatoes are cooked.

5 Add the vinegar, tomatoes and Chinese cabbage, and simmer for 1–2 minutes. Season to taste with salt and pepper. The dish is intended to provide enough liquid to be served as a first-course broth. This is followed by a main course of the meat and vegetables, sprinkled with the shredded scallions. Serve with rice as an accompaniment.

Poached Chicken

An organic free-range bird is the best choice for this simply cooked dish.

Serves 4
1 leek, roughly chopped
1 large carrot, roughly chopped
1 celery stalk, roughly chopped
1 medium onion, roughly chopped
3½-pound chicken
1 tablespoon roughly chopped fresh parsley
2 teaspoons roughly chopped fresh thyme
6 fresh green peppercorns
Mustard Mayonnaise, green salad and lightly cooked baby carrots, to serve

1 Put the leek, carrot, celery and onion in a large saucepan. Place the chicken on top, cover with water and bring to a boil. Remove any scum that comes to the surface.

2 Add the herbs and peppercorns. Simmer gently for 1 hour. Remove from heat and let the chicken cool in the stock.

3 Transfer the chicken to a board or plate and carve, discarding the skin. (Save the stock for another dish.) Arrange the slices on a serving platter. Serve with mustard mayonnaise, green salad and lightly cooked baby carrots.

Mustard Mayonnaise

This tangy mayonnaise is a delicious accompaniment to poached chicken.

Makes 1½ cups
1½ cups reduced-calorie mayonnaise
1–2 tablespoons Dijon mustard
1–2 tablespoons lemon juice
salt and freshly ground black pepper

1 Whisk all the ingredients in a bowl until well blended.

2 Cover with clear film and chill until needed.

Chicken with Lemon Sauce

Succulent chicken with a light, refreshing, lemony sauce and just a hint of lime is a sure winner.

Serves 4
4 chicken breast fillets, skinned
1 teaspoon sesame oil
1 tablespoon dry sherry
1 egg white, lightly beaten
2 tablespoons cornstarch
1 tablespoon vegetable oil
salt and freshly ground white pepper
chopped cilantro leaves, chopped scallions and lemon wedges, to garnish

For the sauce
3 tablespoons lemon juice
2 tablespoons lime cordial
3 tablespoons sugar
2 teaspoons cornstarch
6 tablespoons cold water

1 Arrange the chicken fillets in a single layer in a shallow bowl. Mix the sesame oil with the sherry, and season with salt and pepper. Pour onto the chicken, cover and let marinate for 15 minutes. Combine the egg white and cornstarch. Add the mixture to the chicken and turn to coat thoroughly.

2 Heat the vegetable oil in a heavy frying pan or wok and fry the chicken fillets for about 15 minutes, until they are golden brown on both sides.

3 Meanwhile, to make the sauce, combine all the ingredients in a small pan. Add a pinch of salt. Bring to a boil over low heat, stirring constantly, until the sauce is smooth and has thickened slightly.

4 Cut the chicken into pieces and arrange on a warmed serving plate. Pour on the sauce, garnish with the cilantro leaves, scallions and lemon wedges, and serve.

Variation
You can replace the dry sherry with white port or dry Madeira, if desired.

Two-way Chicken with Vegetables

This tender, slow-cooked chicken makes a tasty lunch or supper, with the stock and remaining vegetables providing a nourishing soup for a second meal.

Serves 6
3½-pound chicken
2 onions, quartered
3 carrots, thickly sliced
2 celery stalks, chopped
1 parsnip or turnip, thickly sliced
¾ cup button mushrooms, with stalks, roughly chopped
1–2 fresh thyme sprigs or 1 teaspoon dried thyme
4 bay leaves
large bunch of fresh parsley
1 cup whole-wheat pasta shapes
salt and freshly ground black pepper
cooked new potatoes or pasta and snowpeas or green beans, to serve (optional)

1 Trim the chicken of any extra fat. Put it into a flameproof casserole and add the vegetables and herbs. Pour in sufficient water to cover. Bring to a boil over medium heat, skimming off any scum. When the water boils, lower the heat and simmer for 2–3 hours.

2 Lift the chicken out of the stock and carve the meat neatly, discarding the skin and bones, and returning any small pieces of meat to the pan. Serve the chicken with some of the vegetables from the pan, plus new potatoes or pasta and snowpeas or green beans, if desired.

3 Remove the bay leaves and any large pieces of parsley and thyme from the pan, and discard. Set the remaining mixture aside to cool, then chill it overnight in the refrigerator. Next day, lift off the fat that has solidified on the surface. Reheat the soup over low heat.

4 When the soup comes to a boil, add the pasta shapes, with salt if required, and cook for 10–12 minutes or until the pasta is *al dente*. Adjust the seasoning to taste, and serve.

Chicken Kiev with Ricotta

Cut through the crispy-coated chicken to reveal a creamy filling with just a hint of garlic—proof that a lower-fat chicken Kiev can be delicious.

Serves 4
4 large chicken breast fillets, skinned
1 tablespoon lemon juice
½ cup ricotta cheese
1 garlic clove, crushed
2 tablespoons chopped fresh parsley
¼ teaspoon grated nutmeg
2 tablespoons all-purpose flour
pinch of cayenne pepper
¼ teaspoon salt
2 egg whites, lightly beaten
2 cups fresh white bread crumbs
duchesse potatoes, green beans and broiled tomatoes, to serve

1 Place the chicken breasts between two sheets of plastic wrap and gently beat with a meat mallet or rolling pin until flattened. Sprinkle with the lemon juice.

2 Mix the ricotta cheese with the garlic, 1 tablespoon of the parsley and the nutmeg. Shape into four 2-inch long cylinders. Put one portion of the cheese and herb mixture in the center of each chicken breast and fold the meat over, tucking in the edges to enclose the filling completely. Secure the chicken with wooden toothpicks pushed through the center of each.

3 Combine the flour, cayenne pepper and salt on a plate. Place the egg whites in a bowl. Combine the bread crumbs and remaining parsley on another plate.

4 Dust the chicken with the seasoned flour, dip into the egg whites, then coat with the bread crumbs. Chill for 30 minutes in the refrigerator. Preheat the oven to 400°F. Dip the chicken into the egg white and bread crumbs for a second time.

5 Put the chicken on a nonstick baking sheet and spray with nonstick cooking spray. Bake for 25 minutes or until the coating is golden brown and the chicken completely cooked. Remove the toothpicks, and serve with duchesse potatoes, green beans and broiled tomatoes.

Chicken & Bean Casserole

A delicious combination of chicken, fresh tarragon and mixed beans, topped with a layer of tender potatoes.

Serves 6
2 pounds potatoes
½ cup reduced-fat aged Cheddar cheese, finely grated
2½ cups plus 2–3 tablespoons skim milk
2 tablespoons snipped fresh chives
2 leeks, sliced
1 onion, sliced
2 tablespoons dry white wine
3 tablespoons low-fat spread
⅓ cup all-purpose flour
1¼ cups Chicken Stock
12 ounces cooked skinless chicken breast fillet, diced
3 cups brown-cap mushrooms, sliced
11-ounce can red kidney beans
14-ounce can small cannellini beans
14-ounce can black-eyed peas
2–3 tablespoons chopped fresh tarragon
salt and freshly ground black pepper

1 Preheat the oven to 400°F. Cut the potatoes into chunks and cook in boiling salted water for 15–20 minutes. Drain and mash. Add the cheese, 2–3 tablespoons milk and the chives, season and mix well. Set aside and keep warm.

2 Meanwhile, put the leeks and onion in a saucepan with the wine. Cover and cook gently for 10 minutes, until the vegetables are just tender, stirring occasionally.

3 Put the low-fat spread, flour, remaining milk and the stock in another pan. Heat gently, whisking, until the sauce boils and thickens. Simmer for 3 minutes, stirring. Remove the pan from heat and stir in the leek mixture, chicken and mushrooms.

4 Drain and rinse all the canned beans. Stir into the sauce with the tarragon and seasoning. Heat gently, stirring, until piping hot.

5 Transfer the mixture to an ovenproof dish and spoon or pipe the mashed potatoes on top. Bake for about 30 minutes until the potato topping is crisp and golden brown, and serve.

Chicken with an Herb Crust

The chicken breasts can be brushed with melted low-fat spread instead of Dijon mustard before being coated in the bread crumb mixture, if you prefer.

Serves 4
4 chicken breast fillets, skinned
a little oil, for greasing
1 tablespoon Dijon mustard
2 tablespoons chopped fresh parsley
1 cup fresh bread crumbs
1 tablespoon dried mixed herbs
2 tablespoons low-fat spread, melted
salt and freshly ground black pepper
boiled new potatoes and salad, to serve

1 Preheat the oven to 350°F. Lay the chicken breast fillets in a single layer in a greased ovenproof dish and spread with the mustard. Season with salt and pepper.

2 In a bowl, combine the parsley, bread crumbs and dried mixed herbs thoroughly.

3 Sprinkle the bread crumb mixture on the chicken to coat it and press in well. Spoon on the low-fat spread.

4 Bake uncovered, for 20 minutes or until the chicken is tender and the topping is crisp. Serve with new potatoes and salad.

Cook's Tip
Dijon mustard is made from black mustard seeds, spices and white wine. It has a clean, medium-hot flavor and a creamy texture. It is the type most widely used in cooking. However, if you prefer a hotter taste, you could use English mustard or for a sweet-sour flavor, use German mustard. American mustard is very mild and quite sweet.

Chicken in Creamy Orange Sauce

This sauce is deceptively creamy—in fact it is made with low-fat fromage frais, which is virtually fat-free. The brandy adds a richer flavor, but is optional—omit it if you prefer and use orange juice alone.

Serves 4
8 chicken thighs or
   drumsticks, skinned
3 tablespoons brandy
1¼ cups orange juice
3 scallions, chopped
2 teaspoons cornstarch
6 tablespoons low-fat
   fromage frais
salt and freshly ground
   black pepper
boiled rice or pasta and
   green salad, to serve

1 Fry the chicken pieces without fat in a nonstick or heavy pan, turning until evenly browned.

2 Stir in the brandy, orange juice and scallions. Bring to a boil, then cover and simmer for 15 minutes or until the chicken is tender and the juices run clear, not pink, when the thickest part is pierced with a skewer or knife.

3 In a small bowl, blend the cornstarch with a little water, then mix into the fromage frais. Stir this into the sauce and stir over medium heat until boiling.

4 Adjust the seasoning to taste, and serve with boiled rice or pasta and green salad.

> **Cook's Tip**
> Adding a thin cornstarch paste to the fromage frais stabilizes it and helps prevent it from curdling. This is also a good technique with yogurt, which will also curdle if it is added to a dish that is going to be boiled.

Oat-crusted Chicken with Sage

A smooth sauce, lightly flavored with sage, makes a fine contrast to the crunchy oats coating these tender chicken pieces.

Serves 4
3 tablespoons skim milk
2 teaspoons English mustard
½ cup rolled oats
3 tablespoons chopped fresh sage
8 chicken thighs or
   drumsticks, skinned
½ cup low-fat
   fromage frais
1 teaspoon whole-grain mustard
salt and freshly ground
   black pepper
fresh sage leaves, to garnish

1 Preheat the oven to 400°F. Combine the milk and English mustard in a small bowl.

2 Mix the oats with 2 tablespoons of the chopped sage, and salt and freshly ground black pepper to taste on a plate. Brush the chicken with the milk and press into the oats to coat evenly.

3 Place the chicken on a baking sheet and bake for about 40 minutes or until the juices run clear, not pink, when the meat is pierced through the thickest part with a skewer or the point of a knife.

4 Meanwhile, in a bowl, combine the low-fat fromage frais, whole-grain mustard, the remaining sage and seasoning. Garnish the chicken with fresh sage and serve hot or cold, accompanied by the mustard sauce.

> **Cook's Tip**
> If fresh sage is not available, choose another fresh herb such as thyme or parsley, instead of using a dried alternative. Although sage can be dried successfully, unlike some herbs, it quickly loses its volatile aromatic oils and becomes very crumbly and dusty with little flavor.

Tuscan Chicken

This simple peasant casserole has all the flavors of traditional Tuscan ingredients. The wine can be replaced by chicken stock.

Serves 4
8 chicken thighs, skinned
1 teaspoon olive oil
1 medium onion, thinly sliced
2 red bell peppers, seeded and sliced
1 garlic clove, crushed
1 1/4 cups passata
2/3 cup dry white wine
1 large fresh oregano sprig or 1 teaspoon dried oregano
14-ounce can cannellini beans, drained and rinsed
3 tablespoons fresh bread crumbs
salt and freshly ground black pepper

1 Fry the chicken in the oil in a large nonstick or heavy frying pan until golden brown. Remove from the pan, set aside and keep hot.

2 Add the onion and peppers to the pan, and gently sauté until softened but not brown. Stir in the garlic.

3 Return the chicken to the pan, and add the passata, wine and oregano. Season well, bring to a boil, then cover the pan tightly. Lower the heat and simmer gently, stirring occasionally, for 30–35 minutes or until the chicken is tender and the juices run clear, not pink, when the thickest part is pierced with the point of a knife or skewer.

4 Stir in the cannellini beans and simmer for another 5 minutes, until heated through. Sprinkle with the bread crumbs and cook under a hot broiler until golden brown.

Cook's Tip
Passata is a pasteurized, sieved tomato sauce which, unlike tomato paste, has not been concentrated. It has a fine, full flavor, as it is usually made from sun-ripened tomatoes. It is available in bottles and cans at most supermarkets.

Chicken with Orange & Mustard Sauce

The beauty of this recipe is its simplicity; the chicken breasts continue to cook in their own juices while you prepare the sauce.

Serves 4
2 large oranges
4 chicken breast fillets, skinned
1 teaspoon sunflower oil
salt and freshly ground black pepper
new potatoes and sliced zucchini tossed in parsley, to serve

For the orange and mustard sauce
2 teaspoons cornstarch
2/3 cup plain low-fat yogurt
1 teaspoon Dijon mustard

1 Peel the oranges using a sharp knife, removing all the white pith. Remove the segments by cutting between the membranes, holding the fruit over a small bowl to catch any juice. Set aside with the juice until required.

2 Season the chicken with salt and pepper to taste. Heat the sunflower oil in a nonstick frying pan, add the chicken and cook for 5 minutes on each side. Remove the chicken from the frying pan and wrap it in aluminum foil; the meat will continue to cook for a while.

3 To make the orange and mustard sauce, blend the cornstarch with the juice from the orange into a smooth paste. Add the yogurt and mustard, and mix well. Pour the mixture into the frying pan and bring to a boil over low heat. Simmer for 1 minute.

4 Add the orange segments to the sauce and heat gently. Unwrap the chicken and add any excess juices to the sauce. Slice the chicken on the diagonal and serve with the sauce, new potatoes and sliced zucchini tossed in parsley.

Turkey Pastitsio

A traditional Greek pastitsio is a rich, high-fat dish made with ground beef, but this lighter version is just as tasty.

Serves 4–6
1 pound ground turkey
1 large onion, finely chopped
¼ cup tomato paste
1 cup red wine or Chicken Stock
1 teaspoon ground cinnamon
3 cups macaroni
oil, for greasing
1¼ cups skim milk
2 tablespoons low-fat sunflower margarine
¼ cup all-purpose flour
1 teaspoon grated nutmeg
2 tomatoes, sliced
¼ cup whole-wheat bread crumbs
salt and freshly ground black pepper
green salad, to serve

1 Preheat the oven to 425°F. Dry-fry the turkey and onion in a nonstick pan over medium heat, stirring constantly, until lightly browned.

2 Stir in the tomato paste, red wine or stock and cinnamon. Season to taste with salt and pepper, then cover and simmer for 5 minutes.

3 Cook the macaroni in boiling salted water according to the package instructions until *al dente*, then drain. Make layers of the macaroni and the meat mixture in a lightly greased, wide, ovenproof dish, ending with a layer of macaroni.

4 Place the milk, margarine and flour in a saucepan, and whisk over medium heat until thickened and smooth. Stir in the nutmeg, and season with salt and pepper to taste.

5 Pour the sauce evenly on the pasta and meat to cover the surface completely. Arrange the tomato slices on top and sprinkle lines of bread crumbs over the surface.

6 Bake for 30–35 minutes or until golden brown and bubbling. Serve hot with a green salad.

Mediterranean Turkey Rolls

Turkey breast steaks have less than 2 percent fat, and they are very quick to cook.

Serves 4
4 thin turkey breast steaks
2 tablespoons Pesto Sauce
½ cup large basil leaves
½ cup Chicken Stock
1 cup passata
garlic salt and freshly ground black pepper
cooked noodles or rice, to serve

1 Place the turkey steaks between two sheets of plastic wrap and beat with a meat mallet or rolling pin until thin. Spread with the pesto sauce. Lay the basil leaves on each steak, then roll them up. Secure with wooden toothpicks.

2 Bring the stock and passata to a boil in a large saucepan. Add the turkey rolls, cover and simmer for 15–20 minutes or until the turkey is cooked through.

3 Adjust the seasoning and remove the toothpicks. Serve the turkey rolls hot with noodles or rice.

Pesto Sauce

A low-fat version of this Italian sauce is quick and easy.

Makes about 8 ounces
1 cup fresh basil leaves
½ cup fresh parsley sprigs
1 garlic clove, crushed
¼ cup pine nuts
½ cup cottage cheese
2 tablespoons freshly grated Parmesan cheese
salt and freshly ground black pepper

1 Process half the herbs, the garlic, pine nuts and cottage cheese in a food processor until smooth.

2 Add the remaining herbs and the Parmesan, season to taste with salt and pepper, and process until all the herbs are finely chopped.

Turkey Tonnato

This low-fat version of the popular Italian dish *vitello tonnato* is garnished with fine strips of sweet red bell pepper instead of the traditional anchovy fillets.

Serves 4

1 pound turkey fillets
1 small onion, sliced
1 bay leaf
4 black peppercorns
1½ cups Chicken Stock
7-ounce can tuna in water, drained
5 tablespoons reduced-fat mayonnaise
2 tablespoons lemon juice
2 red bell peppers, seeded and thinly sliced
about 25 capers, drained
salt
mixed salad and lemon wedges, to serve

1 Put the turkey fillets in a single layer in a large, heavy saucepan. Add the onion, bay leaf, peppercorns and stock. Bring to a boil and reduce the heat. Cover and simmer for about 12 minutes or until the turkey is tender.

2 Turn off the heat and let the turkey cool in the stock, then lift it out with a slotted spoon. Slice thickly and arrange on a serving plate.

3 Boil the stock until reduced to about 5 tablespoons. Strain and set aside to cool.

4 Put the tuna, mayonnaise, lemon juice, 3 tablespoons of the reduced stock and a pinch of salt into a blender or food processor, and process until smooth. Stir in enough of the remaining stock to reduce the sauce to the thickness of heavy cream. Spoon over the turkey.

5 Arrange the strips of red pepper in a lattice pattern on the turkey. Put a caper in the center of each diamond shape. Chill in the refrigerator for 1 hour, then serve with a mixed salad and lemon wedges.

Turkey Picadillo

Using ground turkey rather than beef for this Mexican-style dish makes it much lower in fat. Serve as a filling for soft wheat tortillas or baked potatoes and then top with some plain low-fat yogurt for a tasty meal.

Serves 4

1 tablespoon sunflower oil
1 onion, chopped
1 pound ground turkey
1–2 garlic cloves, crushed
1 fresh green chile, seeded and finely chopped
6 tomatoes, peeled and chopped
1 tablespoon tomato paste
½ teaspoon ground cumin
1 yellow or orange bell pepper, seeded and chopped
⅓ cup raisins
½ cup sliced almonds, toasted
3 tablespoons chopped cilantro
⅔ cup plain low-fat yogurt
2–3 scallions, finely chopped
4 soft tortillas
salt and freshly ground black pepper
shredded lettuce, to serve
lime wedges, to garnish

1 Heat the oil in a large frying pan and add the chopped onion. Cook gently for 5 minutes until soft. Stir in the ground turkey and garlic, and cook gently for another 5 minutes.

2 Add the chile, tomatoes, tomato paste, cumin, yellow or orange pepper and raisins. Cover and cook over low heat for 15 minutes, stirring occasionally and adding a little water if necessary.

3 Stir in the toasted almonds, with about two thirds of the chopped cilantro. Season to taste.

4 Transfer the yogurt to a bowl. Stir in the remaining chopped cilantro and the scallions.

5 Heat the tortillas in a dry frying pan, without oil, for 15–20 seconds. Place some shredded lettuce and turkey mixture on each tortilla, roll up like a pancake and transfer to a plate. Top with a generous spoonful of the yogurt and cilantro mixture, and serve immediately, garnished with lime wedges.

Mandarin Sesame Duck

Duck is a high-fat meat, but it is possible to get rid of a good amount of the fat by cooking it in this way. (If you remove the skin completely, the meat can be dry.) For a special occasion duck breasts are a good choice, though they are more expensive.

Serves 4
4 duck leg or boneless breast portions
2 tablespoons light soy sauce
3 tablespoons honey
1 tablespoon sesame seeds
4 mandarin oranges
1 teaspoon cornstarch
salt and freshly ground black pepper
lightly cooked snowpeas, carrots and bean sprouts, to serve

1 Preheat the oven to 350°F. Prick the duck skin all over. Slash the breast skin (if using) diagonally at intervals.

2 Place the duck on a rack in a roasting pan and roast for 1 hour. Mix 1 tablespoon of the soy sauce with 2 tablespoons of the honey and brush onto the duck. Sprinkle with sesame seeds. Roast for 15–20 minutes, until golden brown.

3 Meanwhile, grate the zest from 1 mandarin and squeeze the juice from 2 of them. Place in a small saucepan. Mix in the cornstarch, then stir in the remaining soy sauce and honey. Heat, stirring, until thickened and clear. Season to taste.

4 Peel and slice the remaining mandarins. Place the duck on individual plates, and top with the mandarin slices and the sauce. Serve with snowpeas, carrots and bean sprouts.

Variations
If desired, you could substitute black or white poppy seeds for the sesame seeds, satsumas for the mandarin oranges and tamari for the soy sauce.

Udon Pot

A quick and easy Japanese dish, this combines chicken with jumbo shrimp, vegetables and noodles in a flavorful stock.

Serves 4
12 ounces dried udon noodles
1 large carrot, cut into bite-size chunks
8 ounces chicken breast fillet or boneless thighs, skinned and cut into bite-size pieces
8 jumbo shrimp, peeled and deveined
4–6 Chinese cabbage leaves, cut into short strips
8 shiitake mushrooms, stems removed
2 ounces snowpeas
6¼ cups Chicken Stock or instant bonito stock
2 tablespoons mirin
soy sauce, to taste

To serve
1 bunch scallions, finely chopped
2 tablespoons grated fresh ginger root
lemon wedges
cilantro sprigs
soy sauce

1 Cook the noodles until just tender, following the directions on the package. Drain, rinse under cold water and drain thoroughly again.

2 Blanch the carrot in boiling water for 1 minute, then drain.

3 Spoon the noodles and carrot chunks into a large saucepan or flameproof casserole and arrange the chicken breasts or thighs, shrimp, Chinese cabbage leaves, mushrooms and snowpeas on top.

4 Bring the stock to a boil in another saucepan. Add the mirin and soy sauce to taste. Pour the stock onto the noodles. Cover the pan or casserole, bring to a boil over medium heat, then simmer gently for 5–6 minutes, until all the ingredients are cooked.

5 Transfer to a serving dish and serve with chopped scallions, grated ginger, lemon wedges, cilantro sprigs and a little soy sauce.

Index

A
Almonds: nutty chicken balls, 21
Apples: chicken, barley & apple casserole, 68
turkey with bay, Madeira &, 76
Apricots: chicken with, 75
Asian chicken sandwich, 19
Asparagus: chicken & asparagus soup, 15

B
Bacon: chicken, bacon & corn kebabs, 50
chicken liver, bacon & tomato salad, 23
Banana, chicken & pineapple kebabs, 84
Barley, chicken & apple casserole, 68
Beans: cassoulet, 74
chicken & bean casserole, 88
chicken with melting onions &, 75
chicken, bell pepper & bean stew, 70
Tuscan chicken, 90
Bell peppers: chicken, bell pepper & bean stew, 70
penne salad with chicken &, 25
smoked chicken, yellow bell pepper & sun-dried tomato pizzettes, 36
Tuscan chicken, 90
Bitki, chicken, 53
Blackberries, chicken stew with lemon balm &, 73
Boilers, 8
Braising, 10
Bread: bread sauce, 65
Breasts, 8
Broccoli: chicken & broccoli salad, 25
stir-fried turkey with mushrooms &, 61
Buckwheat noodles: chicken & buckwheat noodle soup, 16

C
Cajun sauce, chicken with, 55
Cannelloni: cannelloni al forno, 34
Caribbean chicken kebabs, 82
Carrots: chicken, carrot & leek parcels, 59
Carving chicken: 11
Cashews: glazed chicken with, 45
Casseroles & stews, 10
Cassoulet, 74
Celery, shredded chicken with, 48
Charter pie, chicken, 79
Cheese: chicken broth with cheese toasts, 14
chicken Kiev with ricotta, 87
chicken with herb & ricotta stuffing, 84
penne with chicken & cheese, 29
Chicken-in-a-Pot, 75
Chiles: chicken peri-peri, 40
Chinese chicken soup, 16
Chinese duck in pita, 20
Chinese-style chicken salad, 24
Chinese vegetables, chicken with, 48
Chop suey, duck & ginger, 60
Cider: country cider casserole, 68
Citrus kebabs, 49
Clay-pot chicken, spicy, 186
Cock-a-leekie, 18
Coleslaw: chicken pitas with red coleslaw, 82
Corn: chicken, bacon & corn kebabs, 50
chicken, bell pepper & bean stew, 70
corn & chicken soup, 17
Conchiglie with chicken livers & herbs, 29
Cooking techniques, 10
Corn-fed chickens, 8
Country chicken casserole, 73
Country chicken sauté, 57
Country cider casserole, 68
Cranberries: baby chickens with, 67
Crunchy stuffed chicken breasts, 56
Cuts of chicken, 8

D
Drumsticks, 8
Duck: Chinese duck in pita, 20
duck & ginger chop suey, 60
mandarin sesame duck, 93
roasting times, 11
stir-fried crispy duck, 60
Dumplings: chicken with potato dumplings, 54

E
Eggplant: chicken & eggplant khoresh, 70
noodles with chicken livers &, 28
Eggs: chicken & rice omelet, 22

F
Farfalle with chicken & cherry tomatoes, 30
Fava beans: chicken, bell pepper & bean stew, 70
Filipino chicken, 85
French vinaigrette, 23
French-style pot-roast poussins, 67
Fu-yung chicken, 47

G
Garlic: chicken with lemon & garlic, 21
chicken soup with garlic croutons, 18
chicken thighs with lemon & garlic, 71
Gazpacho sauce, turkey rolls with, 61
Ghiveci, chicken, 74
Golden chicken, 52
Goose: roasting times, 11
Gravy, 11
Ground chicken, 8

H
Ham: chicken & ham pie, 79
penne with chicken & ham sauce, 31
Harlequin rice, 49

INDEX

Herbs: basic herb stuffing, 66
chicken with an herb crust, 88
roast chicken with fresh herbs & garlic, 65
Honey: honey roast chicken, 64
pan-fried honey chicken drumsticks, 51
Horseradish: chicken in creamed horseradish, 69
Hunter's chicken, 57

I
Italian chicken, 33

J
Jambalaya, 37
Jointing a chicken, 9

K
Kebabs: Caribbean chicken, 82
chicken, bacon & corn, 50
chicken, banana & pineapple, 84
chicken liver, 50
citrus, 49
sweet-&-sour, 49
Kiev: chicken with ricotta, 87
Knish, chicken, 78
Koftas in tomato sauce, 35

L
Lasagne: chicken, 34
Leeks: chicken & leek pie, 77
chicken, carrot & leek parcels, 59
cock-a-leekie, 18
Leftover turkey casserole, 76
Legs, 8
Lemon: chicken with garlic &, 21
chicken with lemon sauce, 86
lemon chicken stir-fry, 44
roast chicken with herbs &, 65
Lentils: chicken with herbs &, 72
Lima beans, chicken baked with garlic &, 83
Liver, 8
chicken liver, bacon & tomato salad, 23
chicken liver kebabs, 50
chicken liver salad, 23
conchiglie with herbs &, 29
noodles with eggplant &, 28
pasta soup with, 15
pasta with, 28
Lollipops, chicken, 51

M
Mandarin sesame duck, 93
Mayonnaise: chicken & curry mayonnaise sandwich, 19
mustard mayonnaise, 86
Mediterranean chicken, 58
Mediterranean chicken with turnips, 71
Mediterranean turkey rolls, 91
Middle Eastern spring chicken, 66
Mushrooms: chicken pie with, 77
chicken, shiitake mushroom & cilantro pizza, 36
chicken stroganov, 40
chicken with, 33
hunter's chicken, 57
layered chicken & mushroom potato casserole, 54
pappardelle with chicken &, 30
stir-fried turkey with broccoli &, 61
Mustard: chicken with orange & mustard sauce, 90
mustard mayonnaise, 86

N
Noodles: chicken & buckwheat noodle soup, 16
individual noodle casseroles, 85
udon pot, 93
with eggplant & chicken livers, 28
see also Vermicelli
Nutty chicken balls, 21

O
Oat-crusted chicken with sage, 89
Olives: chicken with, 59
Omelet, chicken & rice, 22
Onions: chicken with melting onions & beans, 75
Orange: chicken in creamy orange sauce, 89
chicken with orange & mustard sauce, 90
mandarin sesame duck, 93

Oven-fried chicken, 56

P
Paella: chicken, 41
Pan-fried chicken, 57
Pappardelle with chicken & mushrooms, 30
Parcels, chicken with herb butter, 78
Pasta: chicken & pasta salad, 25
pasta soup with chicken liver, 15
pasta spirals with chicken & tomato sauce, 32
with chicken & sausage sauce, 32
with chicken livers, 28
with turkey & tomatoes, 35
Penne: penne salad with chicken & bell peppers, 25
with chicken & cheese, 29
with chicken & ham sauce, 31
Persian chicken, 55
Pesto, 91
pan-fried chicken with, 53
Pies: chicken & ham pie, 79
chicken & leek pie, 77
chicken Charter pie, 79
chicken knish, 78
chicken parcels with herb butter, 78
chicken pie with mushrooms, 77
Pilaf, chicken, 39
Pineapple: chicken, banana